I DON'T
WANT TO
GROW UP

Also by Scott Stillman

Wilderness, The Gateway to The Soul

Nature's Silent Message

Oceans Of My Mind

Wilderness Speaks

SCOTT STILLMAN

I DON'T WANT TO GROW UP

WILD
SOUL
PRESS

Wild Soul Press
Boulder, Colorado

Editor: Emma Mure
Copy Editor: Melissa Kreikemeier

Library of Congress Cataloging-in-Publication Data
Stillman, Scott
I Don't Want to Grow Up / Scott Stillman

LCCN 2020924126

ISBN: 978-1-7323522-6-1

To Mom & Dad

For teaching me kindness and generosity.
For showing me "when you give, it comes *back*."

Contents

Preface

My fellow readers...

At first glance, this book may appear as a departure from my nature writing. Upon reading it however, I'm confident you will find it is not. As you might know by now, I find it impossible to discuss any matter without also discussing nature. We are *inseparable*.

So here you go—another nature book. Part memoir, part philosophy, part how-to, part prayer for a better future—but a nature book, nonetheless. You will find it different, yet the same.

My sincere hope is that it finds its way into the hands of someone who's suffering. Struggling to find their place in this crazy world. Struggling to *grow up*.

If it helps a single person, I'll consider it a success.

Thanks for allowing me this opportunity. Thanks for your continued support. My gratitude is boundless.

S. STILLMAN
St. Somewhere, USA

When I went to school, they asked me what
I wanted to be when I grew up. I wrote down "happy."
They told me I didn't understand the assignment.
I told them they didn't understand life.

-John Lennon

PART I

Being Born

The most effective kind of education is that a
child should play amongst lovely things.
-Plato

The Freaks

Some believe in life after death. I believe in life
after birth. And if there is a heaven, it resides
here—on Earth—not in some faraway galaxy in
our imaginations, or if you are good enough, or
if Jesus loves you enough, or if you save enough
money, or if you are *successful*. Heaven exists for
us all—because we were born here.

When we came into being for the first time, in our mother's womb, we floated in ecstasy. We were warm, well-fed, and taken care of—we had everything we needed. Then one day we were born, and our eyes opened up to a whole new and even greater world—albeit scary at first. But once we adjusted, our eyes opened wide with wonder and amazement.

Our natural state was one of awe.

Everything around us moved with life and sparkling energy. Colors were vivid. And the shapes. The sounds! Overwhelmed we were with feelings of joy, delight, fear, and curiosity. Everything was so big and exciting and scary and wonderful. Of course, we couldn't say a word of this to other humans, so we tried to communicate through feeling and with our eyes, but they just couldn't understand, and we couldn't understand why. What we wanted so desperately to say we had no words for—and still have no words for—because what we were experiencing was *pure feeling*.

So today when we look into a baby's eyes and see that same awe, we gasp at its purity.

We are born knowing everything there is to know—we just can't say it. When we grow up and learn to speak, we forget what we wanted so desperately to say.

Deep inside every one of us exists that same child who knows everything there is to know, yet when we tap in, we still cannot put it into words. Our vocabulary is too unevolved, existing on an extraordinarily basic level. Sure, we have long, exhaustive combinations of letters and figures for animals, plants, fungi, bacteria, and so forth, but nothing to describe that overwhelming state of awe we are born into. That state we glimpse when we experience a few moments of mindless thought, perhaps while peering into some vast landscape like the Grand Canyon, or gazing out over the ocean, or while surfing, skateboarding, mountain biking, scuba diving, skydiving, hiking, running, fishing, sailing. We only have one word in the entire English language that even comes close. That word is *love*.

This book is about choosing *love* as your life's purpose. It's about living—beyond all else—and spending your entire life in that childlike state of awe. It's about *never growing up*.

Sound selfish? Childish? Irresponsible?
Well...it is.

This book is about dying and going to heaven—and remembering you are there. I've done my fair share of travel, and I'm here to tell you, there *is* Heaven on Earth. We have wild blue oceans, grandiose mountains, sparkling deserts, dripping rainforests, and otherworldly landscapes with more awe than you could fit into a lifetime. *A lifetime!* This book is about prioritizing *experience* and living out the rest of your days in a continuous state of wonder, curiosity, and never-ending adventure. Sound impossible? Idealistic? Expensive? Solely for rich trustafarian kids born into a life of wealth and privilege?

We are *all* privileged.

Privileged beyond comprehension. To the degree that most of us take for granted our own wealth. Let's face it, if you live in today's America, you are more likely to overeat than starve, more likely to commit suicide than be killed, and your chances of being eaten by another animal are, well—for all intents and purposes—zero.

We can roam about freely with little restriction or limitation aside from our own. Transportation is cheap. We have buses, trains, Uber and Lyft. You can walk, bike, hitchhike, or fly. We were born into the world of Airbnb, couch surfing, hostels, and 640 million acres of public land where you can camp—usually for free.

By the way, those *public lands* just happen to be the most beautiful places on Earth. All of this you inherited, just by being an American.

But please, let's not take this for granted. Countless individuals have dedicated their lives— lost their lives in many cases—so that we could enjoy this *free land*. Battles have been fought, both in the battlegrounds and in the courtrooms, so that you and I could enjoy these basic freedoms. The fight for public land has been a long arduous battle. You can thank Abraham Lincoln, Theodore Roosevelt, John Muir, and so many others before our time.

The real question is—
what are you going to do about it?

How to show our gratitude? By wasting away our precious freedoms working a job we hate, all for the sake of raising children to do the same? Does this sound normal? Well, it should. It's what millions of people do every day.

Let's step back for a moment. Someone has to run the show. Someone has to be the accountant, the lawyer, the factory worker, the dentist, the brain surgeon. Someone has to be *responsible*.

Rest assured—plenty will. Most of these fine individuals would never even consider purchasing a book called *I Don't Want to Grow Up*. They are the "lucky" ones—you know who they are—the ones with drive, ambition, and direction. The ones who were born to be analysts, scientists, therapists. The ones who got good grades in school and were focused and determined to pursue careers with excitement and dedication. We *need* them—and pay them handsomely for their services. And this is all very well and fine and good, but for the rest of us—you know who you are—fidgety in school, distracted, staring out the window at pretty girls (or pretty boys), daydreaming about things you'd rather be doing if you weren't stuck in class, or detention, or whatever predicament you happen to find yourself trapped in at the moment.

I'm simply here to enlighten you that *not growing up* is an option, and it's never too late to start. The world needs you, more than you might think. Don't think of your desire to *never grow up* as a distraction, but as a calling. This isn't about kicking back in your mom's basement playing video games. It's about living the life you were born to live.

This world needs "crazy" people—now more than ever before. The ones on the fringes of society who don't quite fit in. Who don't necessarily subscribe to the Hollywood version of the *American Dream*. They are the dreamers—artists, musicians, adrenaline junkies, nomads, life seekers. Without them, the world would be one cold, stale, miserable place.

The world needs *freaks*. Those who doubt conventional wisdom, question authority, and continually search for newer, better ways to live.

Freaks change the world.

So—if you want a safe, predictable life; if you're pursuing an exciting career in a serious field; if you want to raise a family in a house with a big yard and two cars and work every day for 8 hours, 10 hours, 12 hours, or whatever the new standard is for a *full-time job*; if your idea of the *American Dream* is working in an office and coming home each night to eat, sleep, and repeat—then by all means, read no further. This book is not for you.

We thank you wholeheartedly for your service and dedication. Now please, get back to work before the boss sees you reading a book called *I Don't Want to Grow Up.*

The Big Question

Let's talk for a moment about something serious. Most of us have absolutely no idea what we want to do with our lives. We never have and we never will. This bothers us terribly and on a profound level. We feel useless, disconnected, scattered, unfocused. If we could just make up our minds. About something, about anything! Then we could be happy. The fact is—you will never make up your mind. You will never know what you want to be when you grow up, for one obvious reason— there is simply too much in this big ole world to ever settle on one thing!

In high school, I remember talking about careers with a girl named Suzy. She told me she wanted to be an occupational therapist. "Occupational therapist?" I said. "How do you know?" I didn't even know what occupational therapy was. It baffled me that Suzy could know this information at such a young age. And that she wanted to do this for the *rest of her life*—of all the possibilities!

Not that there's anything *wrong* with occupational therapy. I'm sure it's a very rewarding field. If I ever need occupational therapy, I'll be happy that people like Suzy dedicated their lives to the profession. But at 16 years of age, all I wanted to do was skateboard. And I liked girls. Skateboarding and girls—that was it. Did I want to skateboard for the rest of my life? Who knows? All I knew was that I wanted to skateboard *now*. And whenever I got tired of skateboarding, I wanted to do something else.

On career day, I went to see the school guidance counselor. She had this questionnaire for me to fill out, and then she asked me some questions to help me decide what I wanted to be when I grew up. I filled out the questionnaire and handed it to her. She pondered over it for a bit, then proceeded with her questions. "What are you *interested* in?" she finally asked. I said skateboarding and girls.

"How about *academically?*" she scorned. I told her I didn't like school very much. "Well then, Scott, what do you want to be when you grow up?"

There it is.

The question—THE BIG QUESTION.

The stress. The anxiety. Why should I have to decide? After a long, awkward silence, I finally said I'd like to travel. To this she frowned, scribbled something down in her notes and sent me back to class. Later, when I received my report, my recommended career was *bus driver.*

If "*hates school*" and "*loves girls, skateboarding, and travel*" equals *bus driver,* I had no interest in growing up, or in any sort of career at all. But we get pressured to decide, so we pick a career just to pick something—to fit in—and to make our teachers, parents, and elders happy. Then we wake up to that hysterical alarm clock fifteen years later and wonder: *Why the hell am I so damn miserable?*

Suburban Home

I grew up in suburban Ohio and went to Fairfield High. I don't know if this was a normal thing, but at our high school, fights were all the rage. It's all anyone ever talked about. Story after story of brawls at parties involving swinging cue sticks and noses exploding like ketchup packets, all told with laughter and applause. Fights were the big after-school activity. Secret locations spread around the classroom like wildfire—empty pools, abandoned parks, basketball courts—anything made of concrete where the worst bodily injury could be done. The objective was always the same—get your opponent on the ground, pin their arms under your knees, and beat them senseless. Fights were filmed, circulated, and played at after-school parties. I remember seeing a videotape of a boy who appeared to be unconscious at the bottom of an empty swimming pool. His arms were pinned as his opponent punched him again and again in the face. At one point the boy doing the beating stopped to adjust his class ring—to better leave his mark—before resuming the bloody pounding.

Everyone was watching, cheering, rewinding back to the goriest parts—zooming in, watching again.

There are things in this world I have no place for. Things I cannot digest. I began learning how *not* to feel. To show emotion was suicide—you became prey.

A group of us went to a party hosted by a friend named Carl. Carl was in a different social circle, so we didn't know anyone at the party but him. At some point while we were chatting it up with some girls, Carl went off to get more beer. Before I knew it, my friends and I were being dragged outside. We were the only skaters at the party, so I guess we didn't fit in. Punches were thrown. We fought back, but it was pretty clear we were out-numbered. We had no choice but to run. I remember that night so clearly, running through the dark woods thinking, "What the hell am I running from?" What had we done to anger so many people? Of all the possible feelings, empathy surged through my blood—for all who'd been ostracized for no reason whatsoever, but for the clothes they wear, their race or gender, their religious beliefs or socioeconomic class. I felt the emotion of a hundred million wounded souls. Rather than fear I felt rage—at humanity itself.

These kids we were running from—they weren't considered troublemakers. They were popular at school. The students teachers loved, bragged about, labeled *most likely to succeed*.

If this was what success looked like,
I wanted no part.

On my way home from school another day, I witnessed a kid from my neighborhood get beaten senseless in his own front yard. Afterward, in his half-conscious state, they dragged him across the front lawn and forced him to eat dirt from his family's garden. They left him there with a face full of blood, caked and smeared with black dirt. The reason for the beating? He had long hair. Stumbling to the garage, he retrieved a rifle and began shooting at his fleeing attackers—and anyone else in sight for that matter. I don't think he much cared who got shot. I ran home as fast as I could. He looked like the devil. That day—I believe he was.

Fortunately, it was just a BB gun. If he'd had access to a real gun, perhaps an automatic rifle, I'm not sure how that day would've ended. How many would have been killed? Probably I'd have been shot too. I'm not sure *reason* was high on his list that particular afternoon.

We didn't have school shootings back in those days. I guess no one had ever heard of them. Or no one had access to real guns. Whatever the reason, they just didn't happen.

Later that year, a friend hung himself in his parent's backyard. Another jumped to his death from the top of a water tower. Things were not well on the suburban front. On Sundays, we'd go to church. Everyone from school would be there with their hands folded—praying for their sins. Nothing made sense anymore.

Talking to the adults was not an option. What could they do, go to the principal? This would never work—you'd be singled out. Word would get around and everyone would know. You couldn't go to class. Your whole family would have to move.

Your parents would have to uproot and get new jobs. And besides, I liked my friends, I liked my girlfriend, I liked skateboarding. Why should I let them ruin *my* life?

My world became more and more unrecognizable. I felt like an alien and wanted no part. I began to understand why kids commit suicide, especially at such young impressionable ages. But never once did I consider it—because there was skateboarding. Always skateboarding.

> *"I'm going to have fun...*
> *Even if I have to be miserable doing it!"*
> *-Lance Mountain*

Skate or Die

My first love was concrete. Banks, curbs, parking blocks, handrails, empty swimming pools, loading docks, parking garages. With the advent of skateboarding, our stale suburban world morphed into limitless potential for creativity and fun. It changed the way I looked at things.

I began to see the world as a playground.

My skater friends were a lively, animated bunch—cut from a different mold. A rare breed never even considered for mass production. They had green hair and mohawks and wore trench coats to school. Their look said FUCK YOU to society, and I loved it. These were *my* people. We listened to punk bands like *Minor Threat, Suicidal Tendencies,* and *The Descendents*. My first concert was *7 Seconds*. I'd never seen a mosh pit. Never even heard of one. At school, if I bumped into someone wrong, it was probable cause for a fist fight. Here, complete strangers were pushing, shoving, slamming against each other and no one cared. No one even got offended. If you stumbled and fell, tattooed hands and spiked wristbands reached out from the abyss and pulled you back into the pit. We flowed together like a single organism, a swirling tornado. It was love disguised as chaos. The mosh pit was an outlet for all the rage in the world. It was therapy, and nothing had ever felt so healthy, so pure, so free. From the outside it looked insane, but on the inside, it was peaceful, spiritual. Healing.

We were looking for answers and a place of belonging. The punk scene was anarchy and anti-establishment, but never violence. Everyone was quite concerned with this—that you're there for the *right* reasons. There was no room for egos. This was a different scene.

Behind the veil, there was something even deeper that attracted me to this strange counterculture. The spirit of creativity, a nonconformist ethos, and DIY attitudes. These people were *thinking for themselves*.

Punk bands created their own record labels, with five-dollar concert tickets and ten-dollar CDs sold directly from the band. A business model specifically designed to *stick it to the man*.

We spent all our free time skating. My friends and I would take the city bus and travel to different locations each day, secret skate spots with exotic names like Piggly Wiggly, D.O. Banks, Mt. Healthy Ditch. Or we'd head downtown to an endless wonderland of rails and grinders, slopes and sliders, drops and transitions. To the masses, these were lifeless urban landscapes, but we saw only opportunity. We were like kids in a candy store—and everything was free.

No one had any money. I remember going into Burger King, and the seven of us ordering one small Coke (free refills). We'd share the same cup, passing it around until our stomachs were swollen with carbonation and corn syrup. Then we'd take to the city streets, high on sugar, adrenaline, freedom, and fun. We'd get chased by the cops. There were no official skate parks in Ohio, so street skating was all we had. Apparently skateboarding was illegal, but I think this only added to the fun and excitement. I remember sitting in the back of a cop car, three of us laughing, smirking, telling jokes. They'd threaten to take us to jail, but there was really nothing they could do. After all, we were fifteen. We hadn't stolen anything. We weren't vandals. We weren't on drugs or starting fights. We were playing on wooden boards with wheels. Our only crime—skateboarding.

In our junior year, my friends and I decided to build a ramp. Street skating was a blast, but sometimes you just wanted to skate without getting hassled. Building a half-pipe in our backyard seemed like a pretty good idea. But since none of us had any money, funding would certainly be a challenge. We began skipping lunches, mowing lawns, shoveling snow—whatever it took to buy plywood, screws, Masonite, and steel coping. We worked together as a team, making hardware store runs as needed, working incessantly until the ramp was complete.

No one ever talked about school, or grades, or what we wanted to be when we grew up. All we talked about was skating. And girls, of course—always girls. Most of all, we were about having fun—in the purest sense of the word. Unless it was raining or snowing, we skated. When we couldn't skate, we'd watch skate videos—*The Search for Animal Chin, Shackle Me Not, Hokus Pokus*, and *Streets of Fire*—rewinding and fast-forwarding to all the tricks we wanted to learn. Zooming in, watching again. The soundtracks to these videos were incredible. Pure adrenaline. It actually *sounded* like skateboarding. Not the music itself, but the way it made you *feel*. These bands, they weren't being played on the radio. You had to seek them out. I remember going into the record store and asking the clerk for *The Adolescents, JFA, Firehose,* and *Agent Orange.* They had no idea what we were talking about. The only record stores we had were at the mall. Camelot. Sam Goody. Coconuts. We'd have to order our cassettes from the back of skateboard magazines or beg our parents to drive us downtown to seek out independent shops.

I was becoming my own person—my life was no longer spoon-fed. This was my journey, and I could make it whatever I wanted. This gave me immense freedom as I started to question *everything.*

Mountains

When December storms covered the concrete with snow, some of us picked up snowboarding. Early snowboarding consisted of going to the golf course and glissading down the snowy hills on an old skateboard deck until we crashed into the snow, or an obstacle, or each other. Real boards were hard to find in the Midwest. But when our local skate shop finally got hold of one, I quickly snatched it up. My first snowboard was a Sims Blade, purchased with money I'd made busing tables at our local pizza joint.

Snowboarding was new, and our only ski resort, Perfect North Slopes, didn't know what to do with us. We must have looked like a shitshow in our jeans, flannel shirts, and rubber work boots. Skiing had always been a bit of a gentleman's sport, with things like style and etiquette to be considered. Here we were, screaming down the mountain, aiming for anything that resembled a jump. This wasn't skiing—it was skateboarding on snow. We got yelled at, chased down by the ski patrol, and eventually outlawed from the resort— which was certainly a setback.

But we had bigger dreams.

When our high school ski club announced a trip to Winter Park, my friends and I signed up immediately. This was our big chance—to finally shred some real Colorado snow. Surf some real mountains! One of the most defining moments of my life occurred on that trip. As our Amtrak train rumbled west through the Rockies, I'd fallen asleep listening to The Cure's *Kiss Me, Kiss Me, Kiss Me* album. When I opened my eyes and gazed out the window, I was exposed to a world I thought existed only in dreams.

There was nothing but nothing.

No cities, no houses, no roads, no electrical wires. No concrete, no cars, no buses, no strip malls. No industrial parks, no warehouses, no landfills. Just mountains—an endless sea of snowy peaks racing passed my window that seemed to go on forever. And I fell in love. Head over heels in love for the first time with the Rocky Mountains as Robert Smith sang the words "How Beautiful You Are". It snowed every night on that trip, making it a huge success. And I knew from that moment forward that Colorado would be my future home.

College

High school came and went, and my urge grew stronger to get the hell out of Ohio. But my love for my girlfriend, Valerie, was also growing, and she still had another full year of high school left. Pressure was on to go to college, but I still had no idea what I wanted to be when I grew up. College seemed to be what everyone else was doing, so I started to consider it. My best friend was going to Eastern Kentucky University, which was only two hours away. It wasn't Colorado, but at least it was out of Ohio. Tuition seemed reasonable so I figured, what the hell, I had nothing else going on, and I could still visit Valerie on the weekends.

EKU proved to be the perfect stepping-stone towards mountain life. My roommate and I plastered our dorm room wall to wall with skiing and snowboarding posters of the Rocky Mountains, and we spent all our free time hiking in the surrounding national forests.

My world was shifting—
from concrete to mountains.

I majored in marketing (the major you pick when you have no clue what you want to be when you grow up) and photography (because taking pictures is fun!). My marketing classes were horrifically dull—*big surprise*—so I skipped most of those. Photography, however, proved to be quite stimulating. I excelled, receiving straight A's on all my projects. But what the hell was I going to do with photography? I had no idea.

The following year, Valerie joined me at Eastern, and we spent all our free time hiking and camping in the nearby mountains. It was a wonderful time of freedom, love, and independence. We got jobs at Applebee's—Valerie as a hostess, me as a server. Life was one big party. Everyone at the restaurant became friends, and work was a constant roll of laughter and fun. Each night when our shifts ended, we'd claim a high top near the bar while the bartender sent free pitchers and appetizers our way. I remember thinking I could live like this forever. Life was so easy. My rent—split with two other roommates—was a hundred and fifty dollars a month. We lived downtown, so we could walk to everything, and because we earned free shift meals at work, spent almost no money on food. My life cost practically nothing, and we were having a blast.

During that time, I became good friends with a guy named Marty. Marty was always up for adventure—any day, any hour—it didn't matter. He'd simply nod, grab his sleeping bag, and off we'd go into the great unknown. Our outings were spur of the moment, often leaving after dark, driving through the deep woods in his rusty pickup—towards some secluded camp in the hills. Marty was a Kentucky native, and it showed. His camping supplies consisted of a bunch of old blankets, an army surplus sleeping bag, and his trusty rifle. We'd be driving down some dusty old country road having a casual conversation when suddenly he'd slam on the brakes, pull out his rifle, and start shooting out the window. I'd be freaking out hysterically, trying to figure out what the hell was going on, when he'd calmly look over and say "groundhog" and then drive on. Marty is one of the kindest individuals I've ever known, but he hates groundhogs. I think it's in his Southern blood.

When we finally arrived at camp, we'd build a fire and shoot the shit until the wee hours of the night. Our conversations were largely philosophical. Marty turned me on to books by Napoleon Hill, Dale Carnegie, David Schwartz, and Claude Bristol. We agreed that college was teaching us nothing, so we created our own education. Books like *The Magic of Believing* and *Think and Grow Rich* taught us that life was full of possibility, and you could do anything you wanted with the right mindset. While everyone else was studying economics, we were studying life.

We'd go on long trips for days at a time. On one such occasion, Marty had researched a bunch of old covered bridges he was interested in exploring. He put marks of all their locations on a Texaco road map and wanted to go seek them out. Marty loved old bridges, old antique shops, old barns, old river ferries—anything with history. I proposed the project to my photography professor, and he gave me the green light, excusing me from class for the remainder of the week. We set off at once in Marty's pickup, loaded with canned goods and camping supplies, plus my photography equipment, which consisted of an old Cannon AT1 camera, 50 mm lens, tripod, and several rolls of black and white film. We camped under the bridges, waking early to capture the magical unfolding of morning light. Marty would poke around the old bridges while I shot roll after roll, trying to capture the mystery and essence of the dusty road, the creaking wood, the misty streams running below.

Covered bridges are a dying breed. Built in the 1800s, they were covered to protect the trusses and decks from snow and rain, preventing decay. With the advent of concrete and steel, these rustic old bridges have become obsolete. Soon they'll be gone. They stand like artifacts—gateways to a forgotten time.

We stopped in small farm towns along the way for sandwiches and milkshakes, poking around old thrift shops for antiques and forgotten treasures. One evening we had trouble finding a place to camp, so we turned into an old church, knocked on the door, and asked if we could camp in the front yard. They invited us to sleep inside, but we insisted that we preferred sleeping under the stars. While setting up the tent, a lady from the church brought us out a hot pan of lasagna. I began to understand that most people are good, news only reports the bad, and when I open my mind to all the grace and beauty in this world, magic can happen anywhere.

The trip was a great success, not just because my photography project was well-received, but simply because we had fun. Fun was the goal. Fun has always been the goal. Because he who has the most fun wins.

If I wasn't camping with Marty, I was backpacking with Valerie at the Red River Gorge or the Big South Fork. We were falling in love more and more each day. We'd make love with the sunrise, fix coffee on the porch, and backpack every weekend. Our apartment was on top of Apollo's Pizza, and we could walk downstairs anytime we wanted to shoot pool or have a couple beers by the jukebox. Old town Richmond was full of history and charm. We'd stroll through town, poking around old buildings and in and out of antique shops. The town was small enough that we knew everyone at the local restaurants and bars. Life was good— but school was low on our priority list. Tuition began to seem like a big waste of money, so we quit college altogether. We could have stayed in Richmond forever, we were happy there.

But we had bigger dreams.

We wanted to move out West but needed to save up some money first. So, we packed up our belongings, headed back north to Ohio, and got married. Then we started looking for work.

PART II

Learning To Live

Every child is an artist.
The problem is how we remain an artist
once we grow up.
-Picasso

Early Trials and Tribulations with Money

Using the success secrets from *Think and Grow
Rich,* I set my first goal to make $100,000. The
goal must be *specific*—said Napoleon Hill. I
knew college wouldn't get me there, so I decided

to go into business for myself. The only problem was, I had no idea what kind of business I wanted to run. Just that I wanted to make $100,000. That seemed like a nice round figure, and at the time I didn't know anyone who'd made that much—except for my Uncle Bill. I'd always looked up to my Uncle Bill. He'd been one of the only family members to go out on his own, and I respected that. His business model was simple: vending machines—soda machines, snack machines, coffee machines—stuff like that. So, I called him up in North Carolina, and he agreed to let me come see his operation and pick his brain about the mechanics of the vending industry. I'm forever grateful for that experience. After a one-week visit, I had a pretty good idea of how the vending business worked and was ready to start my own back in Ohio.

I'd keep the plan simple, just like my Uncle Bill's. I went through the business section of the phone book and called upon businesses that had more than 500 employees. When I got the receptionist, I asked who was in charge of the vending machines. When I got that person on the line, I asked them two questions:

1. Are you happy with your vending machines and service?

2. Would it be alright if I followed up in a few months to make sure you're still happy?

Before long, I had a large tickler file full of names that I called upon daily. I was building relationships, and the business owners were impressed with my tenacity. Eventually I acquired accounts. I traded in my old college beater for a van, paid for my vending machines with a credit card, and stocked the machines myself.

I was doing well, making my credit card payments, and on my way to running a successful business—all without a college degree. I was proud of myself. I'd found success. But soon it all began to feel like just another job. Did I really want to deliver snacks for a living? Is this how I wanted to spend *my life*?

I began to question my motives. So what if I can make $100,000 if I have no free time to enjoy it?

Sure, I could hire people to stock the machines, but how long would it take to reach that point? With the sizable amount of debt I'd accumulated, it could take years. Was this the lifestyle I wanted? Was this how I wanted to spend *my youth*?

I panicked. A month later I sold the company, paid off all my debt, and became a free man once again.

> *"If the first plan which you adopt does not work successfully, replace it with a new plan."*
> *-Napoleon Hill*

I knew I didn't want to stock vending machines for a living, but in the process, I'd learned something else—I was pretty good at sales. So I decided to try my luck as a salesman. If our goal was to move to Colorado, I figured I'd need to make the most money possible in the least amount of time. Sales is actually a bit like owning your own business, only you're selling someone else's product, there's no overhead, and you can bail out anytime you want. Basically you eliminate the risk.

I went to the classifieds, scanned the sales and marketing section, and much to my surprise, found dozens of ads. Many proclaimed you could make $100,000—no college required. Amazing! How had all these opportunities slipped right under my nose this whole time?

Though I had no documented sales experience, I applied at Toyota and explained my role as "CEO" of my vending company. They seemed reasonably impressed, offered me the job, and said I could start Monday morning.

My first day at Toyota was—interesting. I can't say I quite fit the mold of *car salesman*. Here I was, an introvert, surrounded by a bunch of loud and boisterous characters with huge personalities. And these guys complained—a lot. About sales, about life, about everything! It didn't take long to realize why these salesmen weren't selling any cars. They talked too much—way too much. They'd talk themselves right out of their sales. Here were their customers, ready and willing to buy a shiny new automobile, and these salespeople would just keep talking. Talking, talking, talking. They'd talk their buyers right out the door!

This meant opportunity for a quiet guy like me, so quickly I developed my *own* approach. I'd treat this just like the vending business. I formulated a few essential questions, and let the client do the rest of the talking. It went something like this:

1. Would you like to buy a car or truck?

2. Two doors or four?

3. Light color or dark?

4. Cash or finance?

So on and so forth. Guess what happened? I never "sold" a damn thing. I asked questions—*they* bought the cars. In no time I was top sales-man. Again, I'd found success. I was amazed how much my college education had paid off—not my classes—but the books Marty and I had read. *The Power of Positive Thinking* was working! I simply used the principles, set my goals accord-ingly, and to my amazement, they worked. Why on Earth weren't these books required reading in my marketing classes? Why weren't they required reading for *life*? I quickly began to realize that with this knowledge—I could do anything. If I just put my *mind* to it.

As soon as we could qualify for a mortgage, Valerie and I bought a house. Right about then, my sales manager/mentor at Toyota announced he was leaving. He told me he was going into the mortgage business. Immediately, I said I was coming with him. I knew nothing about loans, but since we'd just purchased a house, I figured I sort of understood the process. "How hard can it be?" I asked him.

A week later he called, offering me a job as *loan officer*. Instead of cars, I learned how to sell loans, and again things went well. Before I knew it, another five years had gone by—and we were *still* in Ohio. I sat down with Valerie, and again we talked about our big plans to move to Colorado. We'd created a pleasant life together in Ohio, saved up some money, but we just didn't fit in. Our neighbors all had kids. Conversations at social gatherings always revolved around children, which was understandable, but we had no plans of having any of our own. Not that there's anything wrong with having kids, we just didn't see the need. We figured the world is already over-populated, and besides, we had other goals, like exploring the American West. We'd saved enough money, our debts were paid—it was time to stop procrastinating. It was time to GO.

One snowy day in February 2003, we packed up our belongings, loaded them into a U-Haul truck, and headed west towards Colorado. We'd researched a lot of towns, and Boulder seemed like the per-fect home base. Around Boulder were endless hiking trails, plenty of jobs, and in our backyard, the tall and majestic Rocky Mountains. Enough exploration to last a lifetime. Not to mention the surrounding wilderness in Utah, Wyoming, New Mexico... So many mountains and deserts. My mouth watered just thinking about them.

After we got settled, I went looking for a job. Again, I used what I'd learned from Napoleon Hill, but I set a different intention this time— *part-time job, full-time pay*. Valerie and I had moved to Colorado to spend our time in the mountains, *not* the office. I knew this was some pretty out-of-the-box thinking, and I had no idea how I'd find such a job, but I figured I'd just trust the process and see what happens. I went to the sales and marketing section of the newspaper, and again found lots of ads, but what piqued my interest the most was one about life insurance sales: *Work from home, leads provided, 100% commission.* The ad claimed you could make $100,000 in the first year. I called and booked an interview. I figured if people were making $100,000 full-time, perhaps I could make $50,000 part-time. I didn't tell this to the insurance company, I just applied for the position and they offered me the job.

Each week they emailed me leads—people who'd filled out a form requesting life insurance—my job was to call the leads, set in-home appointments, and write the policies. Simple enough. Valerie hadn't accepted a job yet, so I offered to split the position with her—essentially turning one full-time job into two part-time jobs. She agreed, and the plan worked flawlessly. In the evenings, Valerie would make the calls and I'd drive to the appointments. During the day we'd go hiking, skiing, mountain biking—whatever. We worked about four hours per day each and earned well over $100,000 in our first year. Did the insurance company complain? Hell no! While the other agents were complaining about low commissions and exhausting hours, we were having the time of our lives. We were independent agents, there was no boss to answer to, and we could schedule time off whenever we wanted. Not to mention—we were making plenty of money.

Later that year we bought our own place, and I began traveling. Apparently, there was a lack of agents in the exploding markets of Las Vegas and Reno, and my manager asked if I was interested in doing some travel. I agreed and again our lifestyle changed. Keeping my ultimate goal in mind—*part-time work, full-time pay*—I structured our business in such a way as to suit our lifestyle. Valerie booked the appointments, and I'd travel to Nevada twice a month for four days. Part of the incentive for traveling was that I'd get as many leads as I wanted. We'd literally book thirty appointments in four days—it was insane!

Our income went up, and so did our free time. We were now working just eight days per month and spending the rest of our time playing in the mountains. Thank you, Napoleon Hill! Again, I couldn't believe how my "college education" had paid off. It seemed that all we had to do was visualize what we wanted, take the necessary action steps, and *voilà*—our dreams came to fruition.

It's Not About the Money

We began to believe we could do anything. But it seemed Napoleon Hill got something wrong. Something big—MONEY. Why had we been making *money* the goal? Why would the goal *ever* be money? Money is worthless on its own. There are plenty of people with lots of money who are miserable. The goal cannot—*must not!*—be money. It must be a question. The most important question of all:

What do you want your life to look like?

We never wanted money. We wanted to backpack, ski, mountain bike, and kayak. To do that we needed *time*—okay, and a little bit of money.

I've never understood the mentality of work hard now, then retire when you're sixty-five. Sixty-five? What the hell am I going to do when I'm sixty-five? My body will never be in better shape than it is *now*.

The time to live can never be later.
It must be now.

We began simplifying our lives by eliminating debt and spending our money on travel and outdoor gear, rather than cars, home furnishings, and electronic gadgetry.

I lost interest in the insurance gig, hung up my license, and enrolled at the United Bicycle Institute (UBI). I'd always had a secret fantasy of becoming a bicycle mechanic. As an avid mountain biker, I wondered what it would be like to truly understand the mechanics of this complex piece of gear I spent so much time with.

The subtle nuances of the drivetrain, suspension, and hydraulic braking systems. What would it be like to intimately know this incredible piece of equipment that feels—at times—like an extension of my own body? Not to mention that working on *toys* didn't exactly sound like a bad way to make a living.

I graduated from UBI, got a job at University Bicycles in Boulder, and went from a six-figure income to fifteen bucks an hour. Here's the funny part—I never even noticed. I know that sounds ridiculous, but it's absolutely true. Instead of buying bigger, more expensive things, we stayed true to keeping our lives simple. Because we had no debt and very few bills, we no longer *required* much income. It was a bit like retiring. You know, it's actually quite common for someone to work a job they dislike for twenty, thirty, forty years— then retire and get a lower-paying job doing something they actually *enjoy*. Why the wait? How many people could sell their homes and belongings, pay off their debts, move into a small apartment, and get a lower-paying job doing something they enjoy—right now? Life is short and money is just money; you can't take it with you—so why are we so obsessed with it?

With as much money as we can make,
can it ever buy back youth?

The switch to the bike shop was perfectly timed. The job was a blast—if you could even call it a *job*. With a little perk called *pro-deals*, employees got new bikes each year. It worked like this: Bicycle manufacturers wanted us riding all the latest gear, so they'd give shop employees wholesale pricing—50% off retail. We'd ride our bikes for a year, then sell them at the end of the season—again for 50% off retail—roughly the same price we'd paid. With the money from the sale, we'd buy another bike. Here we were, essentially a bunch of punk kids getting paid to work on toys, riding nicer bikes than our corporate clients. I felt like we'd cracked some kind of secret code.

Did money even matter?
Or was it really all about *lifestyle*?

Everyone at the shop became great friends and we went riding every day. It was a lot like the old skateboarding days—just a group of friends hanging out, telling jokes, and laughing our asses off all day long. It was a blast. This wasn't work—this was fun.

We were getting *paid* to have fun.

Another three years came and went. We went on countless mountain bike trips to Moab, Fruita, Sedona, and Crested Butte. When I wasn't mountain biking, Valerie and I were backpacking the Rocky Mountains and the deserts of Utah. When winter snow covered the peaks, we'd ski the backcountry, staying overnight in ski huts, enjoying cold winter nights beside the warmth of a blazing fire. Photography was still a passion, but I'd also started writing. I created a website called scottstillmanblog.com and posted photos and essays of our travels. As the blog gained followers, I began to take writing more seriously.

Again, Valerie and I sat down at our kitchen table and began planning our next *big adventure*.

Sell Everything

What would it be like to sell everything and hit the road for a year—maybe longer—maybe even write a book about the whole thing? It seemed like the next logical step in our "career." We called up a realtor to list our home, and what do you know—it sold. The rest came together rather quickly. We gave away most of our belongings, except for a few essential items that we locked away in a storage unit. Then we moved into a small truck camper I found on craigslist and hit the road.

And the rest, as they say—is history.

"Life's a dog and then you die. No, no, life is a joyous dance through daffodils beneath cerulean blue skies. And then? I forget what happens next."
-Edward Abbey

It's amazing how things fall into place when you know exactly what you want. Before I knew it, we were chugging down the highway in our truck camper, in search of the *New American Dream*. I wrote about that trip in my first book, *Wilderness, The Gateway to the Soul*.

Some things you plan, others you don't. I never intended to be a writer—we were just having fun. I started writing for the hell of it—for my own amusement—and if someone actually happened to *read* it? Jumpin' Jesus on a pogo stick—what a bonus! I self-published *Wilderness, The Gateway to the Soul* in September 2018, and it proceeded to sell 20,000 copies in the first six months. I was astonished. It seemed the more we simplified, the richer we became. I'm not talking about money— I'm talking about life. The ability to do what we want, when we want.

My dream of *never growing up* was actually coming to fruition.

How many people suffer, trying to figure out what they want to do with their lives? I've known quite a few—myself certainly included. I started to wonder, could I write a book about not growing up, not choosing a career path, and simply living for the sake of living? How many are suffering in this very moment, struggling to contort themselves into a mold they'll never fit? Is the career-less path really so bad? Could it actually be—*a calling*?

How many are fighting a battle that can never be won? Is it so bad to simply have fun?

I Don't Want to Grow Up

What does it mean to grow up? Many things, to be sure. For me, it has always meant giving up on your dreams and facing *reality*. But whose reality? When we're young, we have dreams as big as the world. Then, when we're older, we're told to *face reality*—as if our dreams and reality are in direct conflict.

We need intention. We need goals. Otherwise, we just sort of sleepwalk through life. What's important to realize is that a goal can be anything.

One goal might be to become CEO of a large corporation, or make a certain amount of money, or reach a certain level of status. Whatever the goal is, it's essential that the *why* be as important as the *what*. Why do you want to be CEO? Why do you wish earn that specific amount of money? Or reach that level of status?

Oftentimes, the *why* is completely unrelated to the *what*. Let's say you want to earn a certain amount of money so you can travel. If *travel* is your desire, why not make *travel* the goal? More important are the details. Where do you want to travel? For how long? A few weeks? A few months? Full time?

What do you want your *life* to look like?

Start there. When you start focusing on *the life you want*, rather than *what you think will get you there*, you're on the right track.

It all starts with waking up in the morning. Visualize your perfect day from morning to night. Where do you live? What are you wearing? What activities are you engaging in? How about a year from now? Five years from now? Ten? Use your imagination and write your story—as only *you* can write it. Adaptations can be made along the way. There are no rules. Everything is subject to change. It's *your* journey.

Once you have your perfect life on paper, with as many details as possible, then—and only then—can you start making a plan. Most people go about this in the exact opposite way, making plans without ever asking themselves *what they actually want*.

Planning

Planning can be great fun, sometimes even as fun as the goal itself. When I'm not traveling, I've got maps spread out all over my living room floor. I mull over them with a guidebook in one hand, highlighter in the other. I'm constantly mapping out new adventures. Go buy some decent maps—you know, the *paper* kind. Your smartphone GPS may be a useful tool, but it lacks the mystery and romance of an actual map. With maps, the world becomes alive again.

You start to see there's so much to explore that you could never fit it into a lifetime. So hurry up—time is of the essence. We only live so long. No one knows when you're going to die, so you'd better get busy *living*.

Why not do something amazing?

In the end we are equal—like the birds, the snakes, the rats, and the worms. We are born with nothing. We die with nothing. It's what happens *in between* that counts.

You are alive now.
That's what matters.

Your heart is beating. Will it beat tomorrow? Who knows? Life is a mystery, and it's time to start treating it that way. The only irresponsible thing you can do is waste it. You are here—God only knows why—but you have the dreams and desires you do for a *reason*.

The truth is—you *do* know why you're here. The problem is society wants your dreams to fit into some preconceived mold. It all goes back to that high school guidance counselor...

"What do you want to be when you grow up?"

Whoever said we wanted to grow up?
Growing up is killing us!

Refusing to grow up is choosing to live—and experiencing every day with the playfulness and curiosity of a child. When we stop seeing the world as a playground, nature as a classroom, beauty in the mundane—we *perish*.

Growing up is like dying and going to heaven, enjoying it for a while, then deciding that all this holiness is a bit dull and we should get on to more important things. As we concern ourselves more and more with these so-called *important things,* we distance ourselves even further from the heaven we were born into—until we forget we're there.

Let me clue you in on a little secret.
Shh. Don't tell anyone...

You're in heaven now.

Heaven on Earth

Watch a small child and you will see that she's in paradise—until her parents insist that she's not. Try and teach her that she's not in heaven. Explain that when she dies, she'll go to a place far better than here. We know the results of such discussion. "Nooooo, Mommy! I don't want to die! I want to live here!" Inevitably, this is followed by tears, tears, and more tears. It's not until we grow up and find ourselves miserable that we desire an afterlife. Some hope beyond this dull, monotonous dread that's become our reality. When we get old, death starts to seem like a pretty good idea—and it should. For in death the cycle repeats itself, and we find our heaven once again.

"Unless you turn and become like children, you will never enter the kingdom of heaven."
-Matthew 18:3

Heaven is full of rainbows, butterflies, sunrises, sunsets, flowers, and bunny rabbits. There are unfathomable mountains, deserts, oceans, and plains. God created this paradise, not so we could destroy it by cutting down the forests, damming the rivers, polluting the oceans, clouding the skies, and drowning out holy wilderness silence with the noise and clamor of industry. We are here to frolic on the hillsides, dance with the flowers, run with the squirrels, sing with the songbirds, and play with the dolphins. We are here to *love*—not just other humans, but *everything* on this planet. We are Earth's children. The mountains, oceans, forests, and animals—they are our kin. They are here for us, as we are for them.

The love in all our hearts is *the same.*

But all this gets obscured. Our regimented society insists life is not a bed of roses, money doesn't grow on trees, and you must work hard for a living. We buy into this, eating the forbidden fruit, forgetting the Garden of Eden. Paradise is stolen—and placed in some imaginary future that exists only in our death.

How did this happen? How did we become so naive? The time has come to *wake up* and start having some fun!

Rest assured, this is not a religious book. I'm not a religious man. I'm not here to preach—only reinforce your own beliefs. If you're an atheist— *this life is all you have.* If you're a Christian— *you'll find heaven when you die.* If you believe in hell—*you'll find it.* We can make our lives a living hell if we so desire. That's the whole point. It's up to you.

Infinite Intelligence

We may have differing opinions about religion, but I think we can all agree there exists a certain kind of intelligence that organizes the universe. The intelligence that allows blood to flow through our veins, bees to pollinate flowers, birds to fly south, salmon to spawn, whales to migrate, caterpillars to become butterflies, Earth to rotate, the moon to orbit, and the rest of nature to function perfectly of its own accord. For the sake of this discussion, let's call it *Infinite Intelligence.* We might also call it *God* or *the universe.*

The key to living the life you want is tapping into this Infinite Intelligence. Each of us has access to this mysterious organizing force, but unless we know what we want, it cannot help us. Most people have absolutely no idea what they want, so the universe cannot help them.

You must have *definite purpose.*

That's the fun part! What does *not growing up* look like to you? Backpacking the Himalayas? Paddling Norwegian fjords? Skiing the Alps? Surfing the Maldives?

What do you *want*?

Start there. Just be careful with dreams like *drink margaritas by the beach*. That can be fun for a few days, perhaps even a few weeks, but eventually, you may need to find something a bit more...sustainable. Equally important is focusing on what you *do* want, not what you *don't*. *Escaping* cannot be the goal. You must know what you are escaping *to*.

What crazy dreams did you have as a kid? What got stifled when *life got in the way*? Those dreams still exist. You just need to reignite them. It's time to do a little soul searching. You may be surprised what lurks deep down in the depths.

Once you know what you want, you can start taking the necessary action steps. When Valerie and I decided to travel the American West, we got very detailed. We knew we wanted to travel for a year, live in a truck camper, and camp for free on public lands. We knew our daily activities would include hiking, backpacking, mountain biking, and kayaking.

Once we had those details in place, the action steps presented themselves quite naturally. The plan was rather simple—sell house and belongings, purchase truck camper, quit job, hit the road. Okay, so there were a few other details, but our main agenda was pretty cut and dry. When plans get overly complicated, too many things can go wrong—we get overwhelmed, we procrastinate. That's why it's best to keep things as simple as possible.

Breadcrumbs

When you know what you want, the whole world changes. Life turns into a magical game of coincidence with clues around every corner. You go on just as before, but you're *aware* of opportunities as they arise. Infinite Intelligence is on your side.

Life throws you breadcrumbs. If you're serious, you follow them. They lead you where you want to go. Always be on the lookout for breadcrumbs. This is Infinite Intelligence conspiring to get you what you want.

At first, your breadcrumbs will be small. Infinite Intelligence is just testing the waters, to see if you're for real. Ignore them, and you send the message that you're a fraud—and your breadcrumbs will disappear. Follow them, however, and it's astonishing where they will lead.

Valerie and I talked about moving to Colorado for years. But it wasn't until we made the *decision* to move that things really started lining up. First, we bumped into a high school friend we hadn't seen in years. It just so happened he was living in Denver and invited us out for a few days (Breadcrumb #1). We ended up finding a great apartment in Boulder, but couldn't move until we sold our house back in Ohio. While searching for realtors in the phone book, I called up a property management company by mistake (Breadcrumb #2). I hadn't considered *renting*, but I decided to follow the lead anyway. The agent on the line informed me a young couple has been searching for homes in our very neighborhood (Breadcrumb #3)! After setting up an appointment, this couple agreed to move in just two months later, paying us $600/month over our house payment. With no jobs lined up, the arrangement created a much-needed income stream for our move to Colorado (Breadcrumb #4).

It's almost scary how the universe conspires when you know exactly what you want. Some people start following these breadcrumbs, only to become scared out of their wits when they see where they might actually lead. Many people are not ready. If you say you want change but flee every time it comes knocking, the universe will get the idea that you're not serious. If you're not serious, you better not start. If you are serious, you better get ready. Change often comes faster than you could imagine.

Begin at Once

This is crucial. Do not wait for the perfect plan. *Do those even exist?* You can improvise as you go. It could start with an invitation to visit a friend or relative you haven't seen in a long time. Or a job opportunity in some other state or country. Sometimes you just have to give the universe a little nudge, especially if you've been ignoring your breadcrumbs for quite some time. It could be as simple as driving a different route to work or taking the bus or train to a place you've never been. There is magic just outside your comfort zone. See what happens when you interrupt your routine, even just a little.

Friends and Relatives

When Valerie and I first pinned Boulder as our goal, everyone said it was too expensive. Naturally, we believed them and started looking elsewhere. After three days of searching the surrounding suburbs, we'd found nothing.

Then we thought about it. We were moving to Colorado to live near the mountains, not suburbia. It suddenly became obvious why we weren't finding anything. We were searching everywhere except our actual goal! So, on the fourth day, we finally decided to check out Boulder proper. Driving down Highway 36, we were immediately entranced by the majesty of the Flatirons—jagged rock formations towering high above town, and the endless hiking trails that flowed right from the neighborhoods. *This* was where we wanted to be. After driving around for just a few hours, we found some affordable housing right at the base of the mountains that was nicer (and cheaper) than anything we'd seen in the burbs!

A similar thing happened when we decided to build a simple mountain cabin. When we went to our local bank, the lending manager told us we couldn't get a construction loan. He told us "only rich people build mountain homes." He actually said that! A couple days later while surfing the internet, a banner ad popped up on my screen for a low-interest construction loan. *Yes, the internet knows everything...* Regardless, I applied online and to my amazement—was approved! What would've happened if we'd listened to that bank manager? Or everyone who told us Boulder was "too expensive"? We would've never moved to Boulder, never built that mountain cabin, never *sold* that cabin which financed our year on the road—never wrote the book that started this whole crazy writing gig!

THE GREAT BIG LESSON:
Don't let anyone influence your dreams.

When you decide to start living the life you want, people call you crazy. They try to talk you out of it. Tell you it's unrealistic. Even impossible. This is usually your family and close friends. It's not that they don't love you or don't want you to be happy. They're just protecting you—at least they think they are—and you can't really blame them for that. But you've got to protect yourself from all that negative energy. It will sabotage your dreams in a heartbeat. The best thing you can do is tell as few people as possible about your plan.

Don't tell them.
Show them.

You've got to be the captain of your ship. This is your life. Your dream. Want to live by the sea and surf every day? Want to ride or hike or sail around the world? Climb every mountain? Live in Alaska? Move to another country? Live in a van? There are people doing all these things—right now. You just don't hear about them. They aren't on social media *posting* about their lives, they're busy *living* them. You'll find them on the backroads of life, the fringes of society, away from all the skepticism and doubt of our mainstream world—quietly living their dreams *anyway*. They don't care what you or I think. And they shouldn't. It's none of their business.

The question to be asking is—
if they're doing it, why can't we?

Are they smarter? Luckier? Have a better upbringing? A better education? Anyone can come up with
a thousand reasons why they *can't* do something.
Only a few go out and live their dreams *anyway*.

PART III

Breaking The Rules

The fool becomes a sage
when letting himself be free to be a fool.
-Alan Watts

The Prescribed Life

We are taught to believe there's only one way to
live. One set of rules to follow. Many define this
as the "prescribed life." It goes something like
this:

School

Job

House (debt)

Family

Consumerism (more debt)

Retirement

Death

Or some variation of that. *Not growing up* means breaking those rules and rejecting society's unwritten laws about how we should live our lives. It's about writing your own story. Sure, this can be scary, but for others, nothing is more terrifying than the alternative.

Don't you have to work hard to be successful?

Not at all. Hard work usually leads to more hard work. Working smart is the key to *not growing up.* When Valerie and I returned from our year on the road, the last thing we wanted was regular jobs. But we were running low on funds, so we started driving for Uber. In our particular market, it didn't take long to realize that all our income came from airport rides. If you've ever been to the

Denver International Airport, you've probably noticed that it's out in the middle of *nowhere*. It's a long ride out there and another long ride wherever the next passenger is heading. Do that a few times a day, and it's pretty lucrative. Valerie and I quickly made business cards with *Airport Rides* printed on the front and passed them out to every airport passenger. We kept our car clean, played good music, and were courteous drivers, so it didn't take long to build a large clientele of business travelers who enjoyed the convenience of scheduled rides, with the luxury of dedicated drivers. We ran all our business through the app, so Uber wasn't in the position to complain, but instead of driving aimlessly around Boulder hoping for airport rides, we worked by appointment, making a full day's income in just a few hours. The rest of our time was spent playing in the mountains. When winter came, we got really serious by setting an ambitious new goal:

Ski every day it snows over eight inches.

Not growing up means prioritizing lifestyle. Arranging work to fit your schedule, not the other way around. We are all busy. We all have obligations. When we prioritize our dreams and follow our hearts, we begin to move past the problems that keep us stuck and toward the life we want.

Not growing up is about resourcefulness and self-reliance. If books aren't selling, I can drive, or work in sales, or repair bikes, or do something altogether different. Why should we ever stop trying new things? Life is an adventure. When you simplify, you can do just about anything. This is freedom in the truest sense of the word.

Freedom is living life on *your* terms. We live in a country that provides this opportunity, which should never be taken for granted—but what good is freedom if we rarely use it? Never before has there been such opportunity to live the life of your dreams. Never before have there been so many ways to earn a living. Never before have there been so many ways to have fun! We are capable of rewriting society's unwritten rules and maximizing these truly unique times. It just takes a little *focus*.

Focus

Many of us have minds that are constantly clouded with a thousand concerns, most of which we can do nothing about. If you pay attention to social media or watch the news, on any given day you'll find an endless sea of things to worry about. I'm not saying you should turn your back on all the problems in the world, but if you're not actively *doing something* to help these problems, what good is it to worry about them? Everybody has the power to change the world. Nobody has the power change *everything*. Try this and you'll go insane!

We must narrow our focus.

We all know people who watch the news incessantly and have something new to complain about every day. Does complaining actually *do* anything? Does complaining help or just add to the world's problems? If we cannot change *all* the things that bother us about the world, why not start with one issue? Something you're passionate about?

Let's say you want to save the rainforests. What if instead of ranting on social media about the ruthless slaughtering of trees, you got involved in an organization that *does something* about it? Let's say you want to end world hunger. Instead of sulking at home thinking about the misery of starving children, why not get involved in a project that *feeds* them? Complaining and ranting does nothing but promote fear and negativity. *Do something*—and live by example. If enough people did this, we might actually make some real progress.

We *are* what we focus on.

Because of this, we're going to need to think about our dreams—a lot. I do this by surrounding myself with books, magazines, and guides of all the places I want to explore. I'm constantly reading travel narratives, drooling over glossy photos, and researching all the exotic places I want to go. This creates a *burning desire* deep down in my soul.

When dreams are charged with desire,
they become *unstoppable*.

Last spring, I injured my foot and my knee. With both hiking and mountain biking off the table, this could easily have turned into "the summer of no wilderness." But rather than sulking in my misfortune, I merely transitioned to kayaking and paddleboarding—and spent the entire summer floating rivers and paddling the ocean. Not to mention writing this book. Nothing can keep me from wilderness because it's *that* important. If this doesn't send a crystal-clear message to the universe—I don't know what does.

Whatever we focus on becomes energized. If we focus on our problems, our problems become energized. They get bigger, more complex, all-consuming. Focus on all the reasons you can't do something, and those reasons will reinforce themselves. Focus on the fact that you're depressed, and you'll become more depressed. Focus on what's wrong with the world and you'll find more that's wrong with the world. This kind of thinking can easily become a never-ending downward spiral of negativity and doubt, leading to depression and mental illness. Even suicide.

You see—we think the universe is so complex, but it's actually quite simple. It gives us precisely what we think about.

Humans are blessed with a wonderful thing called *free will*. Our destiny is up to us. We just need to *decide*. The way to let the universe know what we want is by focusing our intention. Animals do this naturally. A squirrel focuses on the nut, so it gets the nut. A bird focuses on the worm, so it gets the worm. You get the gist.

Humans, on the other hand, do not operate so simply. Rather than focusing on the nut, we focus on all the *problems* that could go wrong trying to obtain the nut. This confuses the universe very much. When we get caught up in this kind of neurotic thinking, the universe actually thinks we want more problems. So that's exactly what we get—more problems.

Why not focus on the nut?

I know this sounds terribly oversimplified. But like it or not, it's how the world works. We are what we focus on—it's *that* simple. We all know people who say things like "problems follow me like a black cloud" or "I can't catch a break to save my life." As we know too well, these one-liners seal their destiny.

The same is true when we're asked how we're doing. When we say "not bad," that's exactly the kind of life we get—*not bad.* I used to work for a guy who, whenever asked how he was doing, would reply each time with the same phrase, "another day, another *struggle*." And it was.

I have this friend who can't get his mind off fly fishing, and he fishes all the time. Another can't get his mind off rock climbing, and he climbs constantly. Others can't get their minds off work, and boy, do they work! But if you spend all your time thinking about work, it's not fair to complain you have no time for fly fishing. The same is true that if you spend all your time thinking about rock climbing, it's not fair to complain you have trouble holding down a job. You see, the universe is giving us *precisely* what we focus on.

What more could we want?

Let's say you're in a bad relationship. And you spend all your time thinking about how bad this relationship is. What do you think will happen? You guessed it—you'll continue having a bad relationship. But let's say instead you focused on your *desire* for a good relationship. A subtle yet not-so-subtle variance. Now you'll likely improve the relationship you're in or leave that relationship for a better one.

See the difference?

All it takes is a shift in the way we do things. A shift in our *perspective*. Most of us blunder through life lost in a swarm of mindless thoughts and ideas crashing into each other all at once. It's no wonder so many of us are on anxiety medicine. When we lived in the woods, things were much simpler. When we were hungry, we focused on food—and we found food. When we were cold, we focused on shelter—and we found shelter. When we were lonely, we focused on love—and we found love. Food, shelter, love—that's what we needed, and the universe willingly provided.

If it had not, our species couldn't have survived.

Now that we've removed ourselves from these cycles of nature, most of us take these basic necessities for granted. Things like food, water, and shelter have become trivial concerns for the typical American. With our bare necessities met, we don't really know what we want, so we focus on the fact that the Joneses have a nicer car, or they travel more, or have better paying jobs. We focus on all the problems in the world by watching CNN or FOX News, or listening to talk radio, or devouring whatever pops up on the internet. We focus on politics, how the left or the right have lost their minds. We divide ourselves up into groups, labeling each other as good or bad based on our affiliations. We learn how to hate— our own brothers and sisters—simply because they're on the other team. We start wars, killing for reasons we cannot readily explain. "It's complex," we say.

Is it?

Is life really so complex?

Turn off the news. If you're focused on everything that's wrong with the world, you're doing more harm than good. You may mean well, but you're part of the *problem*.

Want to save the manatee? Stop complaining and go to work for an organization that saves manatees.

Want to save the wilderness? There are projects that need your help—right now.

If you've read my other books, then you know of my deep love for Utah's redrock canyons. Unfortunately, these pristine deserts are under constant threat from oil and gas development, unnecessary road construction, and rampant off-road vehicle use. When writing my first book, I decided to dedicate an entire page to the Southern Utah Wilderness Alliance (SUWA), an organization that helps protect these fragile landscapes. This was a "baby step." I didn't know if anyone would even read the book. After all, I was an unknown author. How was I to possibly know it would reach *thousands* annually?

The point is—start with something. Anything. Turn your life into an experiment. Take "baby steps." They often lead to bigger ones. That's been the formula for anyone who's ever made a difference.

Focus on what you *want*,
and you might just make a difference.

Perhaps even change the world.

Vibration

As most of us learned in elementary physics, everything in the universe is made of matter and energy—including ourselves. Energy vibrates at different frequencies. The lower our vibration, the closer we are to death. Think of the heartbeat...

When our dreams are charged with passion and emotion, we vibrate at extremely high levels. This gives us a direct link with Infinite Intelligence— the birthplace of creativity, the source of all life. However, we cannot maintain this frequency very long if we are not physically healthy. This means eating the right foods and exercising on the regular.

Fast food, ice cream, and Doritos are not going to sustain us. Junk food only brings our vibration levels down. Many have found that a low-sugar, high-fat diet, rich with whole foods and vegetables works pretty well. Find what works for you. I'm no nutritionist—but most would agree there's nothing worse than sugar. Only certain animals can even taste sugar, and most won't even touch it—it has no nutritional value to them. Interestingly, it's one of the most highly addictive substances for humans, and millions are addicted.

It starts at our first birthday party—with cake and ice cream. Then Frosted Flakes and Cocoa Pebbles for breakfast. Kool-Aid. Popsicles. Gummy Bears. No wonder we're so addicted. We were doomed from the beginning.

The best thing to do is get rid of it.

Sugar leads to obesity and diabetes and mental disorders like depression and anxiety. Nothing zaps vibration levels quite like sugar.

Naturally, when you give up anything as highly addictive as sugar, there's a period of withdrawal.

But once you come out on the other side—what a relief! A new kind of sustained energy takes over, mood swings become a thing of the past, and you begin to live life on a more *even keel*. Try it for a week and see for yourself. Replace sugar with something delicious. Coffee. Tea. Nuts. All good replacements. When you stop eating sugar, you may find that hunger in general diminishes. That's because what most of us perceive as hunger is actually a craving for sugar. Get rid of the sugar and you'll likely find that you eat less food overall. It's quite empowering to get a hold of your appetite. Many are slaves to their food without even realizing it. How liberating to take back your life and eat when you *want*, not just when you feel famished?

We've all felt that insatiable hunger that demands food *now*—this instant! It comes on like a drug addiction. Certainly, insatiable hunger makes sense if we haven't eaten for a few days—it's nature's way of keeping us alive. But when we experience insatiable hunger just three hours after our last meal—that's not hunger—that's a sugar crash. Nix the sugar and take back your life.

It's about interrupting your routine and insti-
gating change. Small changes lead to big ones.
Show the universe you're serious. That you're
willing to take the necessary steps and make
the necessary sacrifices. You'll be surprised how
your life changes as a result.

Just as important as eating is exercise. No diet
will keep you healthy on its own. You've got to
move. Let the body know you wish to live at full
throttle by running, swimming, climbing, cycling,
dancing. Whatever gets you moving!

When we're exercising, not only are we healthier,
but we vibrate at exceedingly high levels. This
helps us process emotion, which can otherwise
stifle our sense of clarity. Daily exercise invokes
creativity, which helps steer your ship in the right
direction. Now throw in a little adrenaline—and
you vibrate at the *speed of life*.

As mentioned earlier, my daily exercise is mountain biking. I've found that nothing increases my
vibration levels like climbing a steep forest trail
at maximum heart rate, followed by the high

adrenaline rush of a zippy downhill laced with roots, rocks, berms, and drops—all with kaleidoscopic mountain scenery rushing by. My body can no longer take skateboarding, but the modern suspension designs of the mountain bike minimize the stress on my joints—and maximize the fun.

Every sport has a learning curve. First, you must build up the right muscles, lung capacity, endurance, and so forth—it doesn't all start out as bliss. But after a while, you become accustomed to this sort of exercise, and begin to feel as though the body is propelling itself. At this point, you run on autopilot. You're no longer working, but *along for the ride.* This is great fun and highly addictive. Joggers call this the *runner's high.* Before long, you'll want to feel this way every day—seeking out every mountain, every trail—traveling to exotic locations all over the world.

This feeling—it's what keeps me up at night and gets me out of bed in the morning. When our passions become obsessions, life becomes a quest for never-ending fun.

That's what *not growing up* looks like.

Don't be put off if you don't like to hike, or mountain bike, or ski—those just happen to be activities that work for me. Find *your* passion. Find your thrill. Then go live it.

Passions keep us young. They take us all over the world, uniting us with others who share similar interests, leading us on a lifelong journey of hair-raising fun. We meet new friends on the road—at hot springs, campgrounds, and trailhead parking lots. We get invited into people's homes, to cook meals, share stories.

When we're outside exercising daily, life becomes a joyous dance. Flashes of inspiration come a mile a minute, solutions to problems come easily, and every day is filled with joy, laughter, and love. *Love for life*. There's nothing better than loving life. When we love life, we beam love out to the rest of the world at the highest possible vibration—just as the sun beams life to us all.

When the world becomes filled with people who love life—the world will be filled with *love*.

That's how we change the world.

Not by inventing the next gadget, acquiring the most possessions, achieving the highest level of status, or making the most money. Napoleon Hill discovered the secrets to success long ago—but money is just a symbol, just as words are merely symbols—not to be confused with what they represent. Money cannot—and must not—be the goal. Love of money only creates the insatiable desire for more money. This creates imbalance and inequality and causes people to do terrible acts. Things they would never do if not for money. Desire mixed with emotion is indeed a *powerful force.*

If we are not here to enjoy ourselves, why are we here? To work ourselves to death? To squander Earth's resources in the name of progress? To justify evil in the name of profit? To horde all the money and possessions we can get our hands on? Who wins the game of life? He who dies with the most money or the biggest grin?

You cannot *buy* your dreams—
only live them.

When you live your dreams, life becomes rich, full of possibility and boundless potential. If you can maintain this level of vibration every day, you begin connecting with Infinite Intelligence— *all the time.*

Just like the rest of nature.

Nature

Communicating with Infinite Intelligence is natural. It's how nature survives. Look at the other animals. Do you see them lounging around, eating too much, or getting fat? Okay—perhaps our pets. But the rest are out running, swimming, flying, chasing and being chased. Unless they're hibernating or asleep, animals are beaming with energy and exuberance! Exercise and adrenaline are normal, essential parts of everyday life. They send signals to the body that life is good. When an animal becomes sedentary, it sends signals that things are bad. That it's old or sick or starving—that it's time to die. When we are sedentary, we send out those same signals without even knowing it.

Our bodies were designed to hunt and gather, chase after food, and run from predators. Since most of us don't chase after our food anymore, or build our own shelters, or migrate with the seasons, we must find adrenaline and exercise some other way. We've got to mimic the *thrill of the hunt*. The thrill of being *alive*. That's why so many of us get hooked on adrenaline sports. So, unless your goal is to run off into the woods and live like the rest of the animals, you'd better find some other way to let your body know that life is good. That, indeed, it's *not* time to die.

So get outside and play!

There is so much more to exercising than the gym. It can be as simple as stepping out your door and running. Just get your heart rate up. When the heart is beating at its maximum for prolonged periods of time, we vibrate at a high-enough frequency for instinct to kick in. When this happens, life transforms into a magical game with clues around every corner. No longer is life about finding opportunities but deciding which ones to pick. When you start seeing opportunities in every direction, you'll know you're on the right track. They'll be no wrong directions, no wrong turns. All choices are correct—just *choose*.

When experiencing this for the first time, it can be quite humorous. Here we were, stumbling around, wishing opportunity would come knocking—and they were there all along, in every possible direction—except the path we were on. Sometimes it just takes stepping off the trail, out of the rut, into the forest of dreams.

The Golden Age of Fun

Has there ever been a better time to be alive? Once food and shelter are secured, our only job is to play. And the ways to play are endless! We're entering a new era: *The Golden Age of Fun.*

In the last several years, backpacks and sleeping bags have become featherweight, and bikes and skis have reached revolutionary levels. Activities like snowboarding, kiteboarding, and paddleboarding didn't even exist just a generation ago.

New and exciting sports are being invented every day.

The last thing you want to do is skimp on gear. Skimp on other things... Do you really need a $700 TV? A $2000 couch? A $30,000 car! It amazes me how many people complain they can't afford decent gear, then proceed to talk about their $10,000 kitchen remodel. You can have a lot of fun for $10,000. Years of fun!

Now, by all means, if you can afford expensive homes, cars, furnishings, *and* quality gear, keep on truckin' my friend. But for the rest of us, we're going to need to prioritize. Life is about priorities— you must decide what's truly important and what's not. If your passion is photography, you're going to need good cameras and lenses. If you're a surfer, you're going to need good surfboards and wetsuits. When these items wear out, you're going to need replacements. This is *non-negotiable*.

Many people won't think twice about upgrading an appliance, but they will put off a new piece of gear for years. Prioritizing lifestyle means putting off the *appliance*.

Not growing up is prioritizing fun.

The folks I know who travel the world are not rich, at least in terms of money. They've simplified their lives to the point where they have very few fixed expenses. If they have a residence at all, it's usually a small apartment or condo where they can lock the door and forget about it for months. Nothing can cramp your lifestyle like yard work, big mortgage payments, and house maintenance— unless that's what you want. Again, it's about priorities and adjusting your life to fit accordingly.

A very logical,
systematic approach.

I recommend an emergency gear fund, a separate savings account or credit card for unforeseen expenses—stolen bike, broken surfboard, damaged skis—stuff like that. If you have trouble keeping debt under control, a credit card is probably not the best option, so go for the savings account. Either way, my *emergency gear fund* has saved me from the untimely predicament of "busted gear...no cash" on many occasions. The ability to finance a piece of gear for a few months can save you from *sabotaging your lifestyle* for years. Trust me, I've seen it happen. We all know the saying, *life got in the way*. Just be careful not to let your gear fund become a shopping spree for everything shiny and new. I find it's best not to even look at new gear until what I have is no longer working.

To make *fun* your life's purpose, it must dominate your being. What better goal could we have? Many argue that we should be thinking about others, not just ourselves—a righteous mindset indeed. However, just because we think we ought to help others, doesn't necessarily mean we have something to give. Our best teachers lead by *example*. Likewise, we cannot expect to help others until we've found happiness *ourselves*.

I'll Be Happy When...

Happiness lives in the present. No one can become happy. You can only *be* happy.

A prime example:

When I graduate, I'm going to get good job, buy a nice house, get married, and raise a family—then *I'll be happy.*

Another:

When I finally pay off my debt, I'm going to quit my job, sell my house, and start traveling—then *I'll be happy.*

And the too familiar:

When I finally meet the right person and find "true love"—then *I'll be happy.*

Plans like these do not work. You cannot project happiness into the future. It doesn't work that way. Happiness attracts happiness. Longing creates more longing. What we should be asking is: "What would make me happy *now*?"

Start there.
And follow the path of happiness.

What Makes You Happy?

What brings you joy?
What makes you *giddy*?

It might be simple. For me, it was surfing pow-der under a Colorado bluebird sky. That's why I moved out West. Snowboarding—that was it!

Once I got there, I found all sorts of other passions, but it all started with snowboarding. Sometimes it's best to keep things simple. What would make you happy *now*?

What puts a smile on your face?
What makes your heart sing?

These are the questions you should be asking yourself. We can come up with a thousand rea-sons for what makes us miserable—money, job, upbringing, etc. When we focus on what makes us happy, the rest of life's details melt away, fad-ing into the background like some annoying song stuck on repeat. An old story we'd been telling ourselves—to convince us why we *can't* be happy.

You may think this all sounds very selfish. But it's actually quite the opposite. I've met all sorts of coaches, teachers, and counselors trying to "help" people, when they still haven't figured out their own happiness. When we live *our* best lives, only then can we inspire others to live theirs.

If you truly want to help people, find happiness. Is there anything else people are looking for? What greater purpose exists? Analyze any dream, any desire, and you will see that the end goal is always happiness.

Some call this *The Five Whys...*

I want to get a degree.
Why?
To get a good job.
Why?
To make money.
Why?
To buy a nice house, raise a family,
go on vacations, contribute to society...
Why?

To lead a meaningful life.
Why?
To be happy.

Another example:

I want to travel.
Why?
To explore the beaches of the world.
Why?
To become a great surfer.
Why?
So I can teach kids to surf one day.
Why?
To contribute to society.
Why?
To be happy.

You can apply this simple line of questioning to just about anything. Opening a business, starting a charity, running a marathon, skiing to the North Pole.

There are endless variations, but the end goal is always the same. When we boil things down, life is pretty simple. We want to be happy.

It's what we all have in common.

It's why we do the things we do.

Happiness means something different to us all. I cannot know what makes you happy. You cannot know what makes me happy. That's what makes us unique. The problem is we have this one-size-fits-all approach. This explains why the prescribed life—school, job, house, family, consumerism, retirement, death—leads to so much anxiety and depression. That formula works for some, but not for all. We are all different, each with unique dreams and desires. These dreams and desires are what makes the world go 'round. If we all wanted the same thing, life would be pretty dull.

Society is constantly pushing us toward a kind of dreaded socialism that dissolves uniqueness and individuality into a colorless mass. We've seen where such practices lead before. Hitler thought he was *improving* society. So did Stalin and countless others. Throughout history, terrorists, cults, and religions have performed unthinkable acts—thinking they were *improving* the world.

I cannot improve you.

No more than you can improve me.

We are perfect as we stand.

Certainly, there are times when we must fight for what is right. Like when we see our basic freedoms being taken away. Our civil liberties and human rights. I do everything in my power to preserve the wilderness. But to preserve the wilderness, I must also *enjoy* it. The very thing I fight to preserve renews my energy, heals losses, and offers valuable perspective. It's easy to get lost in an endless battle of political debates and forget what we're fighting for in the first place.

Fight for what you believe in.

Live for happiness.

When we stop trying to *control* everything and focus on ourselves, the world will finally function as it should.

Do clouds intend to provide rain? Do trees intend to provide oxygen? Of course not. They do these things selfishly. Similarly, when you live your best life, you help others in ways you cannot imagine. When we second-guess our true nature, we second-guess God.

Why do you think we *have* a true nature?

Suppose the sun stopped shining, deeming itself overly selfish just beaming all the time, not contributing "more" to the world. Suppose bees stopped gathering nectar, feeling guilty "taking" from the flowers. Suppose clouds stopped providing rain, thinking they should help the planet some "other" way.

The world would fall apart.

Nature works *because* it is selfish. It is selfish by *design*. It is we who second-guess our dreams. When we stop following our dreams, we let the whole world down.

The only selfish act
is *not* following what's in your heart.

Evil comes, not from selfishness, but self-righteousness—forcing our set of morals and ideas upon others, coercing them to live or act in a certain way. This causes more pain than anything else. How many of us perpetuate the cycle, with our own feelings of moral superiority toward others, for the way they choose to live or their moral, political, or religious beliefs? How many have been *killed* in the name of self-righteousness?

The most selfless thing you can do
is *love yourself.*

It sounds like an oxymoron, but think about it for a moment. When you say that you love yourself, what do you actually mean? When you describe *yourself*, do you refer to your organs, cells, and tissues? Or do you say that you love trees, or mountains, or dolphins? Or food, or music, or art? Or dogs, or kittens, or children?

What you're really saying is
you love the world.

PART IV

Rewriting The Rules

I never allowed my schooling
to get in the way of my education.
-Mark Twain

Love Comes First

You exist so the universe can experience itself only
as it can through you. Your uniqueness is proof of
that. To fight this uniqueness is to deny the will
of the cosmos. Infinite Intelligence works through
the heart, the place where dreams come from.

Do not mistake these messages as selfish whims or childish musings. They are from the divine.

Follow your heart and a path will reveal itself. I never dreamed of writing books—I just wanted to explore the wilderness. That's my passion, and it's what I've done for decades. I don't care if I have to shovel chicken shit, so long as I can explore the wilderness. That's how important it is.

Though I've never actually shoveled chicken shit, I've worked a whole slew of strange and unconventional professions to stay on the wilderness path. When you make your passion your life, you become an expert at being *you*. Do this long enough and you may just find a way to make a living at it...

Just be careful. Turning your passion into a business can be a trap. When we shift gears to making a buck rather than following our hearts, everything falls apart. The world's greatest artists became that way because their art was never about the money. They did it for love.

Love must come first.

Look at The Grateful Dead. Their music was never about the money. Success eventually came because the music was pure. Music and art stand the test of time when they don't conform, or follow the rules, or adhere to some pre-packaged formula for success. The artists refuse to turn passion into a job.

They refuse to *grow up*.

The Grateful Dead were just goofing around. They never intended their music to be anything else. Their *job* was having fun.

So that's it? Really? The big secret to life— having fun?

Not convinced? Go out into a field and watch a hawk for about an hour. Or paddle out into the ocean and watch dolphins. Or chipmunks in a city park. Or butterflies. Imagine for a moment we could communicate with these creatures. Try to reason with them that life isn't about having fun. Try explaining that they should focus on something a bit more *serious*. Teach them that life is about hard work and discipline. Tell the chipmunks to stop goofing off and start *earning a living*.

What might they say about this line of thought? What might they try to teach us? I imagine it could go something like this...

Silly human, you still don't understand. Life is abundant. Food is everywhere. Earth provides everything we need. It's you humans who have gone mad. You work, work, work, depleting Earth of its resources so you can buy all your crap, with your thing called money. Why are you so obsessed with this money? We animals have no use for it. We can't eat it. We can't make shelter out of it. It's useless. Earth provides everything we need for free. All we need is food and shelter—the rest of the time we play, and we love, and we are exuber-ant! Even procuring food is immensely pleasing to us. We love running, chasing, hunting. This is part of life, and we love it very much. Why would you willingly work eight hours a day, five days a week, fifty weeks a year for money, when all you need is shelter and food? For us, seeking food and shelter is simply a continuation of play. In fact, we never stop playing. We play until we are too old to run, too old to chase. When our bodies finally wear out, it's simply time to move on. When the game is over, we die. But most of us never even make it that far, because when we become weak or slow, we get eaten. And that's part of life too. For when we die, we get to become the eagle, or the lion, or the wolf. Our bodies become food, but we go on. In this way, we never really die at all. We just go on and on. So is the endless dance of life.

We live in heaven all the time, and we love life! But you humans threaten to ruin it for us all, with your endless pursuit of money and power. You are mentally ill and need help. The very thing that can help you the most you destroy. When you destroy nature, you abolish your final lifeline to every-thing true and wild and free. We animals want so desperately to teach you, but we don't know how, so we live by example. We cannot communicate directly, so we show you every day how to live. Unfortunately, many of you have stopped pay-ing attention to us. You constantly stare at your glowing rectangles, even while outside in nature. Or you wear your headphones or sit inside your cages staring at even larger rectangles. It seems that these glowing rectangles are taking over your lives. They've become more important than what is right in front of your eyes. So much even, that you hardly notice the forests being torn down, the rivers and streams being polluted, and the air filled with smog. You just continue working, working, working—so you can buy bigger, fancier, more sophisticated rectangles to distract you even more. We fear that someday you won't even notice us. Then the last of the forests will disappear, and life as we know it will vanish.

All that will be left is your devices, and you will go blind. Blind to truth. Blind to reality. Blind to the fact that you were born in paradise and you gave it up. You sold heaven for profit. Truth for fantasy. Doomed to a life trapped inside your own minds, your silly game.

But it doesn't have to be this way.
There is still time!

Please, we beg of you, don't grow up! Listen to your children. They'll teach you everything you need to know. Stop teaching them, and for once, let them teach you. Children know the secret of life. It's the grown-ups who've forgotten.

Life is simple.
Once food and shelter are procured—
it's time to play!

Or something like that...

I can't pretend to know what the animals might say. All I know from my years of forest wandering is that sparkle in their eyes, that fleeting glimpse that suggests there's still hope for us humans. But we've discussed this before—in *Nature's Silent Message,* in *Wilderness, The Gateway to the Soul*— no need to revisit the whole concept here. This book is about *not growing up*.

To do that, we must step outside the regimen— and learn to follow instinct.

Instinct

It starts with a feeling in the gut. A hunch or a twitch. This is instinct kicking in. We still have our instincts, just like the rest of nature. We've just forgotten how to use them. Follow your instincts, and it's almost scary how well they still work. We never lost them, just neglected them.

When instinct begins to steer your ship, it may seem insignificant at first. Just pay attention to coincidence—this is instinct communicating directly with Infinite Intelligence. When you follow coincidence, exciting things begin to happen. Your vibration increases, leading to more and more coincidence—the pathway to your dreams.

Things literally begin *snapping* into place. Many attribute this to luck or being in the *right place at the right time*. But the truth is, you were in the right place all along. You just didn't know it because you weren't following your instincts.

When Valerie and I set out to build our mountain cabin, we literally just started "driving around." We had no idea *where* we were going to build or *how* we were going to afford it, just that we wanted a mountain cabin. We'd gone through the listings, but there was nothing even remotely affordable. We knew we wouldn't find anything sitting in our living room, so one day we got the urge to just go driving...until we spotted the "land for sale" sign in the brush. The lot was south facing, with big open views of the mountains, and remarkably, it was within our price range. Apparently, the property was for sale by owner. If we hadn't followed our instinct to just go "driving around," we'd never would have stumbled upon it.

Follow instinct and luck becomes your friend, dreams morph into reality, and you never look back. It only takes a few of these so-called *lucky breaks* to convince you that life is easy, dreams are just dreams, and you can do anything.

The problem was never getting what you want. The problem has always been *knowing* what you want. But we get so concerned with the *how* that we forget the *what*.

Forget the *how*.
That's not up to you.

What do you want? Write it down. Plaster it on the wall. Make it an all-out-obsession. When our dreams become obsessions, we vibrate at the level of Infinite Intelligence—the frequency of God.

The universe is *pleading* with you to follow your dreams. But you must make the decision yourself.

What if Martin Luther King didn't follow his dreams? Or Harriet Tubman? Or Susan B. Anthony? How would the world be different?

Resist Conformity!

The whole point is: There's more than one way to live. More than two ways. There are infinite possibilities here on God's green Earth. Why then, would anyone willingly conform to the beliefs of a particular group?

Live your *own* life, form your *own* opinions, and when all else fails—

THINK FOR YOURSELF!

Some have called my ideas political. This couldn't be further from the truth. There's nothing I can't stand more than the right-wing Republican. Except perhaps the left-wing Democrat. I don't know which is worse. Left-wing, right-wing. I say they're all bad. Parasites of society. For to be a right-winger, you must resist the left. And to be a left-winger, you must resist the right. Liberal, conservative, progressive, regressive—why the labels? When we label ourselves, we conform. When we conform, we give up the free-thinking mind.

RESIST CONFORMITY!
EXIST ON YOUR OWN TERMS!
BE YOUR OWN PERSON!

It all boils down to this: We cannot have left without right, any more than we can have front without back, top without bottom, out without in. They're two parts of the *same thing*. They go *together*—like negative and positive, female and male, yin and yang. So why are we so compelled to cling to one side?

When we cling, we're lopsided, harebrained, pig-headed. When we're open, we're objective. Rather than fighting, we *learn* from each other. We find *common ground*.

How interesting that our country is not only divided, but *precisely* divided? This should be no surprise, because *nature* is precisely divided, containing the same amount of negative as positive energy. This delicate division balances us out. And it is perfect.

When we stop clinging, everyone will finally see that collectively—we all want the *same thing*.

We just have different ideas on how to get there. And this is not a *problem*.

The *problem* is we split everything up into groups and pit them against each other, labeling each other as good or bad, creating enemies among ourselves. Somewhere along the line, our great commandment got changed, from

love thy neighbor as thyself

to

love thy neighbor as thyself—
unless they're on the opposite team.

Left and right are opposite poles—they balance each other out. Until we realize this glaringly obvious fact, we'll continue kicking the right foot with the left, until we trip and fall flat on our face.

We need to be thinking of entirely new ideas— based on the laws of *nature*. Our future lies in embracing differences and meeting in the middle. United we stand, divided we fall...

...so on and so forth.

Enough already with politics.
On to more practical matters,
like *earning a living*.

Earning a Living

If I don't grow up, how will I make a living?

That all depends on your definition of *living*. What does *living* look like to you? Too often I hear people say things like "I could never travel like you do. Some folks have to *work* for a living..." But a *living* can mean something different to us all. If your idea of *living* is a four-bedroom house on three acres of land, with two late model cars, modern furnishings, and all the latest electronic gadgetry to keep you entertained, your *living* requires a great deal of income. I have a friend in Montana who fishes every day and lives in a van. He follows the weather to different fishing spots throughout the year, and along the way he takes seasonal jobs working in fly shops, as caretaker of a lodge, or a barista in a coffee shop. When each season ends, he gets in his van and drives away— to the next fishing spot, of course. His idea of *living* requires very little.

There's no *wrong* way to make a living.

When people talk about growing up and getting a *real* job, what do they mean by real job? Usually, they mean more money. But what's the money *for*?

We've come full circle again.
It's not about the money.
It's about the lifestyle.

So yes, you do need to make a *living*. Just be careful not to get sucked into someone else's idea of what that looks like. It's your life and your *living*. So get creative. People are constantly bending the rules of what it means to make a *living*. With your goals in mind, there's no limit to the ways you can make your life work. And there's absolutely no reason you should ever have to get a "real job"— unless that's what you want.

Versatility

To survive in today's world without a career, we must be versatile, adaptable, clever, resourceful. Fortunately, when you live outside the box, it only gets easier to *think* outside the box.

The highly specialized career person has an extremely narrow focus. Let's take the architect, for example. The architect will only work in the field of architecture. If he is laid off, he will only look for a replacement job within his field. If the only job he can find is in Indiana, he'll likely move to Indiana, even if he prefers the ocean or the mountains. If the job requires working sixty-hour weeks, he'll do it—after all, he must make a living. If the job requires him to spend his days in airports, or on buses or subways, or under fluorescent lights, he'll likely do that too.

The noncareer person has choices. At any moment, she can quit her job or switch fields if it doesn't suit her lifestyle. She puts lifestyle first, so everything revolves around her *life*, not the other way around.

The architect would never work at Pizza Hut. He'd consider that insulting, perhaps even degrading. But the noncareer person has no problem with Pizza Hut, so long as it suits her lifestyle. She'd find it degrading to live in Indiana, spending her days in airports, or on buses or subways, or under fluorescent lighting. Pizza Hut is just fine if she's saving up for Thailand, or a season skiing in Crested Butte, or surfing in Baja, or writing her next book. She too is extremely focused, about the *living*, not the career.

See the difference?

The wealthy businessman will argue that with money, he can travel anywhere he wishes. This may be true. Yet often this kind of travel is plagued with phone calls, text messages, conference calls, emails, stockbrokers, meetings, and the general anxiety of being away from the office. He may own properties all over the world—gorgeous homes with picture windows framing lakes and mountains, leather-bound furniture adorning the rooms, fine artwork hanging on the walls—as they sit empty.

If that's your jam, more power to you. This is a free country—that's what makes it great. I'm not here to judge, only enlighten you that making a lot of money isn't the *only* way to travel. Most of my travels have involved living in a truck or a tent. But when I travel, my mind is not preoccupied. I think that's worth something of great value.

Can we place a value on peace of mind?

Simplicity is not the *only* way. There are many ways to enjoy this grand ole world. That's the beauty of it—we get to choose. That's what this book is all about. Your life is your choice and no one else's. You needn't come from a wealthy family, or have grown up in the right neighborhood, or graduated from an Ivy League university. No matter who you are, or what your upbringing, you can live the life *you* want.

You can *never grow up*.

But—just like everything else, *not growing up* takes discipline. It's not an excuse to disengage with the world. You must keep your dreams and aspirations on the forefront of your thinking. Otherwise, the great machine will pull you back in.

A classic example:

Let's say you start working that job at Pizza Hut in November to save up for through-hiking the Pacific Crest Trail in April. Though you only intended to work for six months, during your time of employment you get offered a management position. Now you reason that with the extra pay you could travel even longer, so you take the promotion. They give you a raise, then another. And yet another. Your employees look up to you. You have status and an impressive job title. Perhaps even a benefits package, 401(k), and profit sharing. With all of this, you start to second-guess your shared living situation with three roommates. So, you get your own place, maybe even buy a house. Five years go by. Ten. Still you haven't taken that hike. You turn forty. Fifty. Now you're overweight with bad knees or developed chronic back pain from working long management shifts.

Society will always pull you back in—the force is mighty strong. To resist, you'd better have some big dreams with firm goals. If you plan to hike the

Pacific Crest Trail on April 1—then come hell or high water, your boot better make that first track in the soil on April 1!

That's the definition of taking your dreams seriously. They must be *non-negotiable.*

While saving up for our year-long trip through the American West, I went to work for a small company in Boulder. I was so ecstatic about our upcoming trip that my enthusiasm rubbed off on my clients. This brought in a lot of extra business. When the time came to put in my notice, my manager sat me down in his office. He was very disappointed that I was leaving and even offered me a management position to stay. I told him I was honored and asked him to reach out in a year, and if I was still available, I'd happily consider. To my bewilderment, in exactly one year, he called! Amazing things happen when you put your dreams first. You become the captain of your destiny, and the world becomes your oyster.

This world loves dreamers. Employers love to hire people who are passionate about life. You stand out like a ray of hope in a sea of mediocrity. Your adventures—put them down on your resume. Impress your prospective employers. Make them want to book an interview just to hear your story. People love to be inspired! Just don't tell them about your next upcoming adventure. When it comes time to leave, it should be a surprise. The best scenario is they're disappointed that you're leaving, but willing to hire you back upon your return. You may even find an employer who agrees to hire you back seasonally, on *your* schedule—a kind of symbiotic relationship—the best kind. Then you'll see that life is abundant, opportunities are everywhere, and you can do no wrong with the right mindset.

You must only take that first step
down the trail of dreams.

Go ahead—open your calendar and mark the date of your next big adventure. Don't worry, this can be anything. Mark it for a week from now. Six months from now. A year. Whatever. Just mark something on the calendar. This is your adventure, and it can be anything. A three-day trek through the Canyonlands? A two-week jaunt through the tropics? A six-month trip to Alaska? A year-long journey through South America? I'll leave the details up to you. It's your dream, not mine. Just pick something and set the date.

DO IT NOW.

Stop reading if you have to. Get out your guide-books, your glossy travel magazines, or head to your local library or bookstore—brainstorm. What do you want? Deep inside, I know you already know. But sometimes we must be *reminded*, especially if we've buried our dreams under several years of dust. Rest assured, they're still there.

Dreams never die.

The world is waiting. We are *all* waiting. Just don't settle. Your dream must be crystal clear. Vague goals like *vacation* or *weekend getaway* just don't work. The universe cannot understand them. It's like asking the universe for food. Food? What kind of food? Rice? Oatmeal? Lobster? Why confuse the universe like this? If you want to hike the Swiss Alps, what trail? When will you start? How will you get there? What gear will you need? Write it down. Make a plan. Do it *now*—this instant! Before your dream slips away.

But I have a family to support...

I know some of you are raising families. Spouses, kids, soccer practice—I get it, you barely have time for yoga once a week. But what if you raised your kids by the example of prioritizing your *own* dreams? Always wanted to see the Nutcracker on Broadway at Christmastime in NYC with your sister? GO—*without the kids.* It's your dream after all—not theirs. In the long run, they'll respect you for it. Children learn by observing our behaviors. If we prioritize our dreams, they'll learn to prioritize theirs. What more could we want for our children?

Love to ski but your spouse prefers the beach? Good news! Contrary to popular belief, love is *not* about sacrifice. Or giving up your dreams to raise a family. Healthy relationships involve *embracing* differences and *encouraging* dreams and aspirations—even when not in alignment with our own.

Mountain biking and snowboarding have always been "my" things. Valerie's never had any interest in either. But she *encourages* me to go without her. And in return, I support *her* dreams and aspirations. That's how healthy relationships work. It's not about trying to *change* the other person. It's about finding the perfect balance. If we sacrifice our dreams for each other, we get two dissatisfied parties.

True love is about acceptance and helping each other grow—into the best possible versions of *ourselves*.

Commitment Phobia

Many of us can't get past setting that first intention, for one simple reason—we cannot decide. Cannot commit. Don't think of it as a commitment. Life is not about commitment—that's a myth. Does the mountain lion spend its time debating whether she should pursue the rabbit or the deer? Today she may have a taste for rabbit. Tomorrow, deer. Wednesday, perhaps gopher. Nothing's forever. Just pick something for heaven's sake. The universe does not care if we change our minds. Just don't be wishy washy. If we're constantly in debate about what we want, we send out fuzzy signals. Remember, your signal needs to be clear—crystal clear. Fueled with emotion and desire that vibrate at the level of Infinite Intelligence. Then, and only then, can the universe hear you. If you change your mind tomorrow, that's perfectly fine, so long as you make your new signal as clear as the first. Just be mindful of why you are changing. Did you change because you thought your dream was too big? Too out of reach? Perhaps you should have started with something a bit smaller... The universe knows no distinction between a *big* goal and a *small* one. It's we who judge our dreams, setting the parameters on what we think we deserve.

Jessie Rittenhouse expressed this truth well in her famous poem:

"I bargained with Life for a penny,
And Life would pay no more,
However I begged at evening
When I counted my scanty store;

For Life is just an employer,
He gives you what you ask,
But once you have set the wages,
Why, you must bear the task.

I worked for a menial's hire,
Only to learn, dismayed,
That any wage I had asked of Life,
Life would have paid."

Whatever your goal, you must be able to *conceive* it—must be able to picture it in your mind. It must be so strong that you feel yourself doing it already. Many change their minds just before manifestation. This is the worst thing you can do. Here's the universe, ready to give you the nut, and you say, "I don't want the nut. I want the berry." Perhaps you figured the nut was too far-fetched. Do this enough times, and Infinite Intelligence will see that you're insincere—and you'll lose your lifeline.

Most people are scatterbrained—including me. That's why I write my intention down on the back of a business card. Why a business card? Because it is small, portable, and fits nicely in my wallet where I can see it daily. Intention must be precise— if it can't fit on the back of a business card, it's probably too complex.

Every time I go to the grocery, or pump gas, or open my wallet for whatever reason, my ultimate desire is right there—staring me in the face. The one I want so badly it dominates my existence. The rest of my life revolves around that desire, not the other way around. The image dominates my thinking until it becomes all-consuming. When we begin *obsessing* about our dreams—they come true.

This is how to transform your life.

You may be starting to see that *not growing up* takes some responsibility. It's not all beach parties and bong hits. It takes discipline and guts. I never said this was going to be easy. You're going to have to work at it. Just remember, opportunity exists in *every* moment, even the ones we perceive as *bad* moments. Try accepting each moment like you chose it yourself. Life is a game and clues are everywhere. Ignore them and get stuck. Follow them to reach the next level.

And the next.
And the next...

The Sixth Sense

When we begin paying attention to life's clues, we develop a sort of sixth sense. Instead of thinking our way through life, we *feel* our way through. No longer do we find the need to debate everything. Rather we're *drawn* to what feels right.

With this in mind, it's good to keep plans open and itineraries loose. If every waking moment is preplanned, we cannot act upon our sixth sense. During my wilderness excursions, I find it crucial to rely on the sixth sense. It guides me to hidden water, forgotten ruins, and lost gems I'd never find on prescribed routes, with fixed agendas.

The thinking mind has no idea where the next opportunity lies. It cannot understand the sixth sense, because it uses no words, no vocabulary at all—only feeling. When you know what you want, it's imperative to follow *feeling*. It will guide you the same way bees are led to flowers. When you awaken the sixth sense, every day becomes a mystery, life overflows with abundance, and you can do no wrong. You'll begin to see that the only wrong turns are the ones that go against your sixth sense. If it feels right, it's probably right. If it feels wrong, it's probably wrong.

Just the way nature works—
moving toward the *good*,
and away from the *bad*.

Gratitude

Gratitude lets the universe know it's on the right track, attracting more *good* into our lives—beckoning more breadcrumbs. Because the universe does not initially understand our preferences, it does not know what we perceive as *good* or *bad*. When things begin to happen that we perceive as *good*—if we express our deep gratitude—we plant little seeds. This allows the universe to zero in more precisely on what we want. The more gratitude we plant, the more seeds are sown. In time, the universe becomes finely tuned to our preferences.

Kind of like a computer algorithm.

If you've ever used the music application Pandora, you've experienced something similar. At first, it doesn't really know what music you like. Then, as you hit *thumbs up* for certain tracks, it tunes in to your preferences.

Gratitude is like a *thumbs up* to life.

If you have a delicious meal, but eat without gratitude, the universe has no idea you enjoyed the meal. If, however, you express genuine heartfelt gratitude, not only for the food itself, but the farmers who grew it, the truck drivers who delivered it, the clerk who shelved it, and all the organisms sacrificed to nourish your body—the universe will bring more delicious food.

But it must be *genuine*. Reciting some rehearsed prayer without feeling does no good. When we give thanks out of some kind of obligation or habit— it does not vibrate. True gratitude *vibrates*. You can literally feel it throughout your entire body. When gratitude vibrates, you connect *directly* with Infinite Intelligence.

Modern advertising works this way too. When a company advertises for the first time, they have little idea to whom they are advertising. This produces very few results. Then, as people begin purchasing products, algorithms take note of each purchaser—age, gender, common interests, and so on. After a while, the advertising becomes highly targeted. The algorithm never stops learning.

That's why it's called *targeted* advertising.

Without gratitude, Infinite Intelligence has no idea what to target. That's why so many people are miserable. Misery perpetuates itself, because when we're miserable, we have no gratitude, except for guilty pleasures such as french fries, ice cream, drugs, and alcohol. So, what does the universe bring us more of? French fries, ice cream, drugs, and alcohol.

What should we expect?

Similarly, if your goal is to hike the Himalayas, but when you get there, all you can think about is your job and all the work you'll have to catch up on when you return—you trick the universe into thinking you didn't *enjoy* the Himalayas.

When your dreams are realized, you must be present, surrendering completely to the experience. Taking in the sights, the sounds, the magic, and abundance of it all—with boundless gratitude for the mystery and beauty of life! When we do this, gratitude becomes a powerful force.

While out in nature, I often feel myself beaming gratitude from head to toe—for the fresh air and sunshine, my strong legs and healthy lungs, the trails and all who were involved in building them, and the lifestyle that allows me to do this sort of thing in the first place. Sometimes it's so overwhelming that I'm dumbfounded—by the extravagance of life itself! The gratitude literally becomes *all-consuming.*

Day after day of such gratitude sends crystal clear messages that life is good. And all the universe wants to do is bring us more!

To start integrating gratitude into your life, begin by making a list. Write down everything you're grateful for in your life—you may be surprised how much you can come up with. Then when you're done, spend some time expressing gratitude for each item on your list. Remember, true gratitude vibrates. It starts in the heart, resonating out to the rest of the body from there. Keep going until you feel yourself vibrating from head to toe. Then move on to the next item in your list. Incorporate this into your daily life and watch how things change.

When life becomes a constant expression of gratitude, you'll know the *true* meaning of happiness.

Learning

Now you know the formula—dreams, plus burning desire, multiplied by intense gratitude, equals the *life you want*.

This is the key to *never growing up*, never choosing a career, and living the life of your dreams. Pretty simple. But it takes rethinking everything we've been taught about the way the world works. It takes a little *rewiring*.

The best way to rewire the brain is through *learning*. In our youth, we're constantly learning new things. How to walk, how to talk, how to ride a bicycle. How to add and subtract, solve problems, interact with others, learn a new trade. Then, when we get older, we tend to do the same thing every day.

We *stop* learning.

This is why time "flies" as we get old. Ten years whoosh by and we say, "Where did the time go? It seems like just yesterday that I started this job!" This should come as no surprise, for when we do the same thing each day, our brains have difficulty discerning one day from the next. They sort of just run together—like one long day.

When we're young, ten years seems like a lifetime. High school feels like decades. Elementary school—an eternity! That's because our lives are in constant motion. We're continually learning new things, and the future is this vast ocean of possibility. Everything is so exciting, and the possibilities are endless. We can do anything! Then, as we get older, each day becomes more and more...*predictable.*

"Just fifteen more years until retirement," we say, as we continue our daily grind, only to arrive at retirement old and worn out. Bad knees, bad back, arthritis...

But we can change that—
if we keep learning.

When we learn, life *remains* a vast ocean of possibility. Learning can be anything—a new language, a new instrument, paddleboarding, windsurfing, scuba diving, dancing, baking, painting, gardening.

When we get too comfortable with a certain skill set, life becomes increasingly dull. When we learn new things, the world opens up—and new opportunities arise.

Learn Spanish and perhaps you'll travel to Spain. Learn a musical instrument and join a band. Learn to bake and open a bakery. Get certified in scuba and travel the world. With learning, the world becomes alive again. We recreate ourselves. In a sense—we are reborn.

The body recognizes this, as we send out signals that it's not time to decay, but to *grow*. With learning, we trick our bodies into believing we are young again. For many, this happens late in life, perhaps after retiring from a job of many years. Some of these folks live well into their 80s, 90s, even 100s. It's never too late to begin learning again. Why not start now?

Start planning the next phase of your life. Those who retire without dreams die early. If you want to live a long and meaningful life—never stop learning. Never stop dreaming. Never stop being curious.

PART V

Learning To Die

I'd rather die while I'm living
than live while I'm dead.
-Jimmy Buffett

Dying Before You Die

In Zen teachings, the whole premise is to die before you die. Meaning that when we let go of attachment to the physical world, we relinquish our primordial fears of death. For many, this happens at the end of our days. When everything has been stripped away—we finally find peace.

But if we learn to *embrace* the unknown, rather than fear it, we get to *die before we die*—and live our lives fully.

Life is about taking risks. That's what makes it fun. Fear and fun are interdependent. They make an adventure an adventure. If you enjoy action movies, then you know—

It's not an adventure
until something goes *wrong*.

So get into adventures. Throw yourself into life— live the story. The best problems are the ones we choose.

Good problems?

Hunting for water in the desert. Getting lost in a foreign country. Searching for a hut in a snowstorm. Sure, they're problems, but they're *my* problems. I threw myself into these adventures.

Bad problems?

Traffic jams. Bills. Health problems. Ugh— nothing terrifies me more. I'll gladly take being chased by lightning, frozen fingers in a blizzard, canceled flights in the Caribbean.

My father-in-law worked hard his entire life to retire at sixty-five. When he finally retired, a blood clot to the lung caused his untimely death. He was a great man and an inspiration to us all. He dedicated his life to supporting a family of seven and saved up for the "golden ticket" of retirement. He died almost two months to the day of retiring. His death was a shock and a reminder of the uncertainty of life. We're all going to die. And no one—absolutely no one—can say when.

The way I see it, the only risk we can take is *not* taking risks.

So sign up for that river trip, get lost in Paraguay, miss that flight in Barbados, board that train to who knows where. Adventures are adventures—no matter how big or small. It could simply be a cooking class, or taking salsa lessons, or learning Taekwondo. Anything outside your comfort zone. Small adventures lead to bigger ones. They guide you along the pathway of your dreams.

Start by saying *yes* to life.

Adventure may come knocking much sooner than you think.

Location, location, location

Love to surf but live in Nebraska? Love to snow-board but live in Miami? You're going to have to move—it goes without saying. Want to travel the world? You may have to give up the notion of having an address at all. We need to find our place. We need to find our *people*.

I'm a firm believer that you can live anywhere you wish on just about any budget. Just be careful not to get caught up on the *cost of living*. When people talk about *cost of living*, what they usually mean is *cost of housing*. Yet anywhere you could possibly live, you'll find people in just about every income bracket. Sometimes we need to get a little creative with our idea of housing. How about renting a room in a house, or a studio apartment, or a live/work situation?

What's more important,
the dream or the dwelling?

Wherever you wish to go, just *get there*.
If the desire is strong enough, you'll *find* a way.

You may just need to let go of any preconceived notions of what you really need to survive. Is your dream to surf or live in a house with a yard?

Many have found accommodations in exotic locations as caretakers or working at lodges. There are affordable housing programs to consider. If you want to live in Hawaii—*get* to Hawaii. Just have an open mind once you get there. Remember, nothing is forever. Believe in the process, follow the breadcrumbs, and know that a river seldom flows in a straight line. Trust Mother Nature and she'll guide you along. Throw a tantrum every time something is a little outside your comfort zone, and she'll send you on the next bus ride home. Sauntering through the door in defeat, you'll grumble, "All that *not growing up* stuff is a bunch of woo-woo."

And you'll be right.

> *"People who do not succeed*
> *have one distinguishing trait in common.*
> *They know all the reasons for failure."*
> *-Napoleon Hill*

Surrender

Now that you've thrown yourself into a life of adventure, it's time to surrender and hand the job over to Infinite Intelligence. When we surrender, we let go of any preconceived notions of how we think things should play out. We *let nature take the reins*. This is how miracles happen.

It's when we look back ten years from now and say, "What a wild ride! I could not have *invented* such a story!"

Life works in mysterious ways. When we hold on too tightly, we often sabotage what the universe is trying to provide. There are no straight lines in nature. We just need to know where we're heading and trust the rest to divine unfolding.

No Straight Lines in Nature

Look at a wild river on a map or the contour lines of mountain range or desert canyon. It all looks like chaos. But as we know, divine intelligence is at work. The river wants to make it to the sea, but a straight line is rarely the path of least resistance. Our *ego* might wish to climb mountains, but nature prefers the easy way around.

Suppose the water objected each time the river made a bend, crying "Wrong way! Turn around! Wrong way!" Well now, that would be ridiculous—yet this is exactly how we go through life. That's why we need to trust, beyond a shadow of a doubt, that nature knows the truest path—so long as our dreams are well defined.

So set the controls to your heart's desire, let nature take the reins, and get ready for the bucking bronco ride that life was meant to be. Just be sure your dreams are bigger than your fear of not achieving them. Otherwise, you run the risk of quitting just short of the finish line. There are a lot of blind curves. It can be difficult to know that your goal lies just around the next bend, the next crest, the next ridge.

How many quit just shy of their dreams?

Life is a journey. Destinations are necessary. They keep us headed in the right direction, but between the dream and the destination is life. *Know* where you are going—*trust* the rest to divine unfolding. The uncertainty is what makes it worthwhile. The best stories, as we know, are unpredictable. When the plot is expected—it's a sleeper. When laced with mystery—it's gripping. What kind of story do *you* want? There are no wrong answers. You write the book.

"May your trails be crooked, winding, lonesome, dangerous, leading to the most amazing view...where something strange and more beautiful and more full of wonder than your deepest dreams waits for you— beyond that next turning of the canyon walls."
-Edward Abbey

Pulling Back the Curtain

What we've really been talking about is *pulling back the curtain* and revealing the truth behind the illusion of "everyday life." Because it's all smoke and mirrors—every last bit. On the surface, it's easy to fall for the gag. Just don't forget it's all a game disguised to keep you believing there's only *one* reality.

With so many people around us living the same kind of life, it's easy to get sucked into thinking there's only one way to live. This is nonsense. Just travel to Mexico or Nepal or Morocco or Egypt—quickly you'll be reminded that people live all sorts of ways—and no one way is *right*.

When we travel, we grow. We see the world is diverse. We get the chance to see through the eyes of other cultures, reminding us that our immediate surroundings are not the real world, but a mere fragment of reality. We see that the world is not small but infinitely large. Most of all, we come to accept our own ignorance. As our minds expand, nothing seems impossible anymore, and we regain our childish curiosity.

With travel, we realize that growing up is just another name for copping out, giving up, throwing in the towel. When we're young, the world is mysterious and unknown. When we grow up, we become know-it-alls. Nothing feels new anymore because think we *know* how the world works. This is gibberish. We can never understand the universe any more than we can understand where we came from and where we'll go when we die. Life is a mystery—that's what makes it worth the ticket.

Many people will think this book is woo-woo. A bunch of fluff designed to sell books and get our hopes up about nothing. Yet there are people living the life I've described every day. You just don't see them. They're on some remote beach in Costa Rica, or trekking the jungles of Nicaragua, or climbing sandstone cliffs in southern Utah. They live life on *their* terms and don't give a damn what anyone else thinks. They couldn't care less if we think their lifestyle is woo-woo, or irresponsible, or selfish, or unrealistic. They might have a thing or two to say about *our* lifestyle. But our differences are what make the world go round. They keep life... interesting.

Still, most will not understand. They think the only way to live is the way their parents did. Their neighbors, their friends, and their peers. They think that to live your dreams you must be wealthy. Again, this is gibberish. Yet society sure would like to keep us thinking this way. It keeps the economy in check—the great machine humming. The problem is we are not machines. We are living beings with souls that yearn for life outside the box. Some of us are born with dreams much larger than cogs in an industrial machine. Yet that's exactly how our educational system is rigged. Rather than harboring dreams, we engineer cogs.

"What kind of cog would you like to be when you grow up?" asks the school guidance counselor.

I just want you to know—
you don't have to be a cog.

Some people are meant to be visionaries—stepping outside the regimen and asking, "How can things be better?" "How can we *live* better?"

Is there a higher calling than the visionary? Without visionaries, might we all be cogs?

Whatever your calling—follow it. No matter how ridiculous, how irresponsible, how reckless people tell you it is. It's your dream and your life. There's no *higher calling* than living it your way.

A Lost Generation

Sadly, we are facing the unhealthiest generation of children in the history of the United States. Childhood obesity is skyrocketing, mental disorders like ADHD have become commonplace, and depression has millions of kids hooked on anti-depressants, many with effects as powerful as methamphetamines and cocaine. It's become a public health crisis like no other.

This national epidemic can only be tied to our disconnect with nature and our ever-increasing desire for safety and security. While previous generations enjoyed things like playing in the woods, making tree forts, and building skateboard ramps, the simple act of playing is becoming a thing of the past. In some places, these childhood pastimes have all but become illegal. With the majority of Americans living in metropolitan areas, very few open spaces for childhood play even exist. What little remains is often riddled with rules and regulations—KEEP OFF GRASS. STAY ON TRAIL. NO FISHING. NO SWIMMING. What is this insatiable desire for order? Even our own neighborhoods offer no escape from such mandates. Gated communities and homeowners' associations now often contain rules forbidding things like skateboard ramps in the driveway, forts in the trees, even toys left out in the yard. More and more we're being told to keep it tidy, keep it safe, and keep it *inside*.

Many parents suffer what's known as *stranger danger* paranoia. Worrying constantly that their children will be abducted if they allow them to play outside unsupervised.

This phenomenon has become so widespread that some parents rarely let their children out of their sight. Instead, we keep them inside our homes, or strap them into automobiles, racing from one organized activity to the next, whizzing past 80,000-pound semitrucks at seventy miles per hour. And this is supposed to be *safe*?

Safety is killing us!
And it's killing our children.

Then we complain that our kids spend too much time watching television. Or staring at their phones. Or playing video games.

What *exactly* do we expect them to be doing?

Watch the news and it's easy to believe that child molesters are lurking around every corner, neighborhood streets are riddled with violent crime, and the safest place for children is in the home.

But this is an abstraction of the truth.

You see, to be newsworthy, a story must be *out of the ordinary*. Otherwise, it's not news. Jackknifed semi on Interstate 70—yawn. Store clerk dies of heart attack—forget about it. *Dangnabbit, where's that blasted remote? We need some real news!* It's not that we don't care, but these stories are a dime a dozen. We've become desensitized to this type of news. To hold our attention, we need something a bit more...disturbing. That's why news reporters flock to such stories as homicides, child abductions, and drownings. And in a country of over 300 million, they're bound to find plenty. To the uninformed mind, it would *appear* that things like homicides, child abductions, and drownings are common.

But it's simply not true.

The most dangerous place for a child is *not* outside! It's on the couch. And riding around in cars. But our society creates a *culture of fear* that obscures reality through the media.

There's only one hope of escaping this sea of madness. Turn off the news. Turn off the TV entirely. Get rid of the danged contraption.

Put it out of its misery.

Obesity, depression, and ADHD are a *direct result* our children's separation with the outdoors. Children need firsthand experience with nature. Yet so much of their education has become secondary. Nature has been reduced to a zoo, an aquarium, a stuffed animal. Or whatever can be found in a classroom, or surfing the web, or in a textbook. But learning the name of every tree, every plant, and every rock, can never teach them about the real world. The real world is *outside*. And it must be experienced. To deny this to our children is to deny them a life of joy and meaning. And ultimately—a spiritual connection with nature.

What more could we want for our children?

It all starts with us. To raise happy children, we must be happy ourselves. When we live our lives with passion, joy, and excitement, we inspire our children to do the same.

As a society, we need to take a step back and give our children the space to explore and be creative. Allow them the opportunity to be bored. Remember boredom? As children, what did we do when we were bored?

We invented our own games, created our own toys out of sticks and string and cardboard boxes— whatever was available. Or we played in the sandbox, or in the dirt, or climbed a tree. Being outside changes everything. Boredom breeds creativity. Creativity breeds geniuses.

Television breeds couch potatoes.

Children have a primal need to play in nature. It's where they learn to follow intuition, trust their instincts, and overcome fear. Nature puts things into perspective, so they can deal with their emotions rather than committing suicide or shooting up a school. They learn to trust their feelings, cultivate awareness, and listen to instinct—moving toward the *good* and away from the *bad*. They develop their sense of curiosity and take nothing for granted. They learn to be *amazed*.

Children that spend their formative years playing in nature don't need to be taught about wilderness conservation later in life. It comes naturally. Human nature compels us to protect what we cherish. Nature can help deepen our children's sense of purpose. Some may even become stewards of the land, protecting nature at all costs—for future generations to come.

Simplicity

What holds you back the most—
yourself or your stuff?

Compared to other species, we must look like aliens. It's incredible how much a single human requires to live. If you could put everything you owned on a scale, how much would it weigh? Think about it for a moment—all that crap.

It's excessive. Compulsive. *Maniacal.*

We even call our stuff *crap*—saying things like, "Where did all this *crap* come from?" "Who wants to help me move all my *shit* to my new apartment?" "My basement is such a wreck. There's so much *junk* down there."

No wonder we feel so trapped in our lives. We've literally buried ourselves under a huge mountain of junk! For many, just the thought of loading all that *shit* in a moving van and transporting it even one mile down the road sounds exhausting. Even impossible. Our modern lifestyle ties us down and keeps us from living our lives fully. Not to mention all the *debt* that comes with all those possessions. If freedom is what you crave, there's only one solution to this problem that plagues the masses—GET RID OF YOUR CRAP!

Sell it, give it to the Salvation Army, post it on craigslist—whatever it takes. Humans are hoarders. We collect things. We think these things give us our identities—photos, knickknacks, old furniture, stacked boxes in the attic full of who knows what. Very often a person's abode will reveal their *state of mind*.

Simplify your life. Simplify your mind.

It's incredible how freeing this can be. Sure, it can be scary. Getting rid of stuff can actually feel like we're giving away of pieces of ourselves. Just remember, you can't take it with you. In the end, we die the same way we came into this world— with nothing. Why not experience peace of mind now? *Before you die?*

Try starting with a single item. Then move on to another. Once you get past the initial inertia, you may begin to feel lighter. Just keep going. Continue getting rid of stuff. You may find it becomes an all-out obsession as you become lighter and lighter, freer and freer.

Personally, I've never felt freer than when we left for that first road trip. We'd gotten rid of almost everything—and I could actually name everything I owned. I could even tell you where it was. The effect this has on the mind is staggering.

Two forks, two plates, two coffee mugs. Small box of essential books and maps. Sleeping bag, tent, hiking boots...

Everything had definitive purpose. How nice to be surrounded by intention! All of it fit neatly in our truck camper. We could go anywhere, do anything! The funny thing was, even with all that simplicity, it still seemed excessive. Why should I need all these things while the rest of nature roams freely?

When a bird makes her long journey south for the winter, she carries nothing but her wings. What is this curse that compels us to carry such heavy loads? What is this burden? How did it *happen*? From the outside—we must look like crazy people. Even the homeless push their heaping carts of rubbish. What drives this insatiable desire to hoard? Could we ever go back to living like the rest of nature? Could we ever be *okay* with just ourselves?

Of course not.

We'd freeze to death, get eaten alive by mosquitoes, go to jail for indecent exposure. Yes—we've even gone so far as making it *illegal* to rid ourselves of every possession. Those who've decided to live the simplistic lifestyle walk a fine line in the eyes of the law. Police officers don't like our answers to their routine questions:

"Address?"
"Don't have one."

"Where are you headed?"
"Nowhere in particular."

Answers like these are cause for concern in the eyes of the law. Must we always be heading *somewhere*? Doing *something*? Is it such a crime to have no agenda? Wandering at will in the direction of our choosing? If that's not the definition of freedom—what is?

Might this explain why so many are plagued with anxiety and depression? Could a simple life of freedom exist just beyond the boundaries of our comfort zone? Outside society's *unwritten* rules?

We are capable of rewriting the play.
It just takes a little intention.

The question remains the same—*what do you want your life to look like?* Once you know that, you can begin stripping away all that is not your desire. Finally, when every last layer has been removed, there will be your dream—sparkling like a diamond in the rubble.

Still, many will leave their diamonds buried—working, working, working—trying to save enough money so that someday they can live their dreams.

But freedom doesn't come from piling up a big heap of money. It comes from stripping away, peeling back, exposing what's buried beneath.

Simplify.
And walk into life unburdened.

This is not groundbreaking information. Plenty of people live simple lives. I meet them on the road of life. Fixing cappuccinos on mountain tops. Mixing margaritas on the far side of the world. Living life *their* way. Moving from place to place on *their* schedule. What scares them most? Security. The stable place of employment. Opportunity for advancement. The private office. The steady paycheck. The *benefits* package. The mere mention of such things will undoubtedly send them running as far as possible from society's trappings. They live the way they do for a *reason*. It all started with a burning desire. The desire to be free.

It's normal to crave security. Yet by nature, life is insecure. The only thing we can count on is change—so we must become adaptable. There are plenty of times when *not growing up* sucks. There's a lot of uncertainty. It can be easy to lose focus and get sucked back into the false security of our modern world. Life is unpredictable— especially when you stray from the beaten path.

Not growing up takes courage, and not everyone is cut out for it. Besides, as I've said, not everyone can just be roaming around, living in vans, playing in the mountains, deserts, and oceans. As we know too well, everyone won't. The urge for security is strong. The comforts of houses, cars, climate-controlled offices, and steady paychecks are far too irresistible for the masses.

Yet, I wonder...

If a squirrel were offered an endless supply of nuts in exchange for living in a temperature-controlled box, would he do it? This, I believe, would be an interesting experiment.

How many of these animals would willingly give up their freedoms in exchange for security? My guess is that some would, some wouldn't. The ones who agreed to such terms would undoubtedly enjoy this new life of security for a while. But in time they'd become gluttons, gaining weight, becoming obese, developing health problems. We'd prescribe them drugs, made just for squirrels, protecting them from things like high blood pressure, heart disease, diabetes. When they became depressed, we'd provide them with entertainment. Give them flat-screen TVs with streaming videos of forests and open hillsides with squirrels running about freely. This would work for a while, but eventually they'd become addicted to these videos. Then we'd administer anxiety medication to numb their feelings. In their numbed state, they'd dream of heaven, a utopia of boundless freedom where all the squirrels run free. A paradise found when you die. Eventually the squirrel *would* die, lonely and afraid, dreaming of a heaven that only exists in his mind.

But heaven is *real*.

It existed long before the boxes, the drugs, the false security. Heaven is freedom. And you don't have to die to get there. You've only to set yourself free, leave your cage, and bound off into the wild blue yonder—the place we all belong.

The place where dreams come true.

I can't help but think that when we dream of Eden, we're actually *remembering*—the way things were, before we boxed ourselves in. Somewhere along the line we ate the forbidden fruit, chose security over freedom, and willfully enslaved ourselves to the great machine. In doing so, we gave up our basic freedoms to roam and frolic in the Garden of Eden.

There is a price to pay for security. A hefty price indeed. When we succumb to the temptations of our modern world, we sell our very own souls, all for the false comforts that society provides, on a planet that willfully provides everything we need in abundance. Have we been duped—forgetting it is *we* who are the experiment?

It may be a little late to go bounding off into the forests with nothing but our birthday suits, but certainly there must exist a *hybrid* sort of living. If we cannot escape completely, perhaps we can still live freely, with one foot dipped in society, the other planted in Eden. Maybe it doesn't have to be *all or nothing*.

The truth is, we cannot have society without wilderness. No more than we can have the chicken without the egg. They go *together*—like black and white, good and bad, left and right political thinking.

We can't have one without the other,
because they're two sides of the same coin.

Wilderness

Wilderness is our only hope. Our final lifeline to reality—and everything that is true and wild and free. When the wilderness disappears, there will be no hope left for the human race. Extinction will be the only way. A social experiment gone awry. And the Earth shall go back to the way it was—before we paved paradise and put up a parking lot.

I see no greater cause, no higher purpose than preserving what's left of our wild lands. The next generation depends on us. The future of the human race depends on us.

Together,
we can make a difference.

The Good Fight

What do *you* stand for? What bothers *you* most about the world? We need your perspective—more now than ever before. Will you fight the good fight? Will you join *the movement*?

What movement? *Your* movement!

Whatever it is you believe in—speak out.
Join forces. Amplify. Grow.

Start by living your dreams. Then inspire others to live theirs, and save the world from a bitter end—by influencing one person at a time.

If you can change a single mind, you can change the world. Show us a better way to live. You might just alter the destiny of humankind.

What do you want to be...
when you *don't grow up?*

Enjoy this Book?
Write a Review!

———————

If you've enjoyed my book, the best compliment you can give is writing a review. As a self-published indie author, I don't have the advertising power of a major publishing firm. But you can make a big difference.

Honest reviews help other readers find me. It only takes five minutes, and the review can be as short as you like.

If you'd like to leave a review on Amazon.com, search for my title, click on *Customer reviews*, then click *Write a customer review*. Simple as that.

Thank you very much.

NATURE BOOK SERIES
(4 part series)

Explore the alpine peaks of the Rocky Mountains, the sandstone slot canyons of the Colorado Plateau, and the lush mangrove islands of the Florida Keys in Scott Stillman's Nature Book Series.

Have you read all the books in the series?

- **Wilderness, The Gateway to the Soul**
- **Nature's Silent Message**
- **I Don't Want To Grow Up**
- **Oceans of my Mind**

(books can be read in any order)

Sign up for my mailing list and you'll gain access to:

- FREE PREVIEW of each book in the series
- My ongoing blog posts
- Exclusive photographs
- Backpacking tips, gear checklists, and more

You can sign up for my mailing list at
www.scottstillmanblog.com

SAVE WILD UTAH!

SOUTHERN UTAH WILDERNESS ALLIANCE (SUWA)

SUWA is the only nonpartisan, nonprofit organization working full time to defend Utah's redrock canyons from oil and gas development, unnecessary road construction, rampant off-road vehicle use, and other threats to Utah's wilderness-quality lands. Their power comes from people like you from across the nation who want to protect this irreplaceable heritage for all Americans.

If you'd like to get involved, please find them at **www.suwa.org**

About the Author

Scott Stillman was born in Fairfield, Ohio, and then moved to Boulder, Colorado, in 2003. Wandering mountains, deserts, and oceans, he records his journeys with pen and notebook, writing primarily about our spiritual connection to nature.

Scott is the bestselling author of the *Nature Book Series,* including *Wilderness, The Gateway to the Soul, Nature's Silent Message, I Don't Want to Grow Up, Oceans of my Mind,* and *Wilderness Speaks.*

As our culture continues to remove itself from the natural world, Scott's books provide refreshing insight, showing that there's life outside the regimen—hope beyond the pavement.

He and his wife, Valerie, have lived in a truck camper and worked a slew of unconventional jobs to fund their travels and stay on the wilderness path.

You can find his blog and online home at:
scottstillmanblog.com
facebook.com/scottstillmanblog

If the mood strikes, send him an email at:
scottstillmanauthor@gmail.com

Made in the USA
Columbia, SC
23 June 2023

18851936R00109